The Evolution of a Teacher

by **Larry D. Allen**

Published by Stradella Books

Published by Stradella Books
120 Sylvan Drive
Valparaiso, IN 46385

www.TeacherSupportInfo.com

Ordering Information:

Special discounts are available on quantity purchases by corporations, associations, educators, and others. For details, contact the publisher at the above listed address.

U.S. trade bookstores and wholesalers: Please contact Stradella Books at (219) 508-1155.

DEDICATION

I want to thank my wife and soul mate, Judie, for her love and encouragement and my wonderful family who have given me strength and hope when the journey at times was blocked with confusion, frustration and disappointment.

This reflection of my journey through 30 years of music teaching is dedicated to my spiritual mentors, including: Wesley Runk, Dick Cool, Roger Decker, Bill Harrod, Jack Bowsher, Ken White, Frank Battisti, Galen Kral, Robert Bloom, Humbert Lucarelli, Jack Alexander, Ira Singer, Henry Schoebel, John Hamby, Moshe Paranov, Donald Harris, Glenn Chandler, Jim Gilworth, Bill Eifrig, Michael Kumer, Jim Rubish, Ed Sueta and Kathryn Dearborn.

These spiritual mentors came into my life at the precise moment I needed their help to continue my journey. Their presence in my life's journey began in sequence from 1957 to the present like clockwork. My journey would have stopped if any one of these mentors had not entered my life at the time of their appearance.

TABLE OF CONTENTS

PREFACE

The Evolution of a Teacher is a new, heart-touching E-Book about a teacher entering the fifth decade of his career. Read about the warmth and love Mr. Allen has for his students as he shares with you the life-changing lessons learned from his mentors and students.

The Evolution of a Teacher is the "Larry D. Allen story." A teacher who begins his saga with his near-death experience at age 7, the parade of mentors that came into his life who directed him into the field of music teaching and music performance, and the students who encouraged his visions to improve the quality of music teaching, student learning and music teacher training.

The focus of this book is the spiritual nature of every student and the high level of energy that each student possesses when they enter into the classroom. Mr. Allen reveals these powerful life-changing experiences with his students and the evolution of his teaching.

One of the powerful teachings in Mr. Allen's experience is the internal teacher within every learner, and the importance for each child to listen to their internal teacher. For a student learning to play a new musical instrument their internal teacher is their vocal skills and their listening skills which have been developed since birth. The internal teacher: the vocal and listening skills will help the learner develop their beginning instrumental music skills.

Excerpted from three Purdue Calumet University students' papers:

- This [sic] e-book was very interesting and encouraging. I think the idea of considering all students to be angels is very encouraging...
- He emphasizes [sic] in this e-book the importance of reaching out to each student, regardless of their category, with love, caring, and a listening ear. When a student succeeds in school, the support triangle was in balance. This triangle consists of the student, parent, and teacher...
- This [sic] e-book has to do with multiculturalism in that every student that comes into a teacher's life has different cultural, religious, and family values. Accepting this reality and helping each student progress in their skill development gives everybody a feeling of accomplishment and significance...

Each generation learns from the previous generation. When Mr. Allen is teaching students, his vision is not one of the students he physically sees in the classroom, but his vision is of the students as leaders of the next generation: fathers, mothers, aunts, uncles, grandparents and future leaders who will teach their values to the next generation within each local community.

This vision is so powerful in that each generation can only teach what they know and what they have experienced at each stage of learning. If a child's misses a stage of learning, it is most difficult to go back and fill in that period of loss. Unfortunately, such a loss in their development is passed on to the next generation.

Finally, Mr. Allen sees "the role of the teacher" as "the highest professional calling" of the 21st century in our local communities: parents, grandparents, aunts, uncles, coaches, school teachers and religious education teachers. These "teachers" are the "mentors" and "role models" who continue to influence the souls of our children: the leaders of the next generation.

Quoting from Stephen R. Covey, "The main thing is to keep the main thing the main thing." For our children, learning to love, care for and respect each other regardless of our individual differences is the "main thing."

It is the cultural birthright of every

child in every culture

of every generation to enjoy the

excitement of learning

and the love shared in the

teaching/learning process.

INTRODUCTION

The angels are the many people throughout my life who have affected me spiritually: parents, children, family, mentors, and students in my classes and private music studio. The "spiritual sharing" of ideas by the students are the angelic experiences that have changed my life minute to minute, day to day, and week to week. I began my first year in education in September of 1969 at O'Connell School in East Hartford, Connecticut, and my 30th year was completed in June of 1999 at Kesling Middle School in La Porte, Indiana.

Over the past 30 years of teaching music my increased understanding of what children need from their teacher has increased my ability to prioritize what is important in the classroom and what is not. This revelation has been the joy of my journey. With this knowledge I was able to find love and peace of mind for the longer journey ahead in my professional, private and spiritual life.

Much of what I have learned took every minute of the entire 30 years of teaching to understand and implement. Over this period of time, my spiritual calling to the field of education lead me to many different types of learning and performing environments in the field of music education. During my first 20 years as a professional musician, I was a public school teacher and administrator by day and a classical musician at night performing with the symphony orchestras throughout Connecticut and Massachusetts and teaching privately at the Hartt School of Music.

It was this combination of working daily with people of all ages, performing the great classical literature, and having the opportunity to make a difference in education that kept me very motivated and kept me in touch with my spiritual calling. Although there were many days of frustration and disappointment, my family and colleagues steered me on the right course of action and encouraged me to keep my visions in perspective.

The opportunities to commission original pieces of music literature by composers whom I loved and respected was and continues to be one of my great joys in life. In addition I had the opportunities to implement a variety of new music programs in traditional school music curriculums in local communities in the states of Connecticut, Massachusetts, and Indiana. This effort improved the quality of music teaching and music learning for thousands of students and teachers annually. For me, these improvements in school music programs and in the musical lives of children and teachers were and continues to be the definition of happiness.

My greatest vision was to help teachers help students. I knew that for every music teacher I could help there would be approximately 500 students benefiting from each teacher's growth in knowledge and enthusiasm.

This vision began to unfold into reality in the fall of 1977 with the Fall Workshops of Music Educators at Naubuc School in Glastonbury, Connecticut. The vision grew to the Hartt School of Music in their Summer term program, and expanded nationwide between 1981-1990 to include Hartt School, Central Connecticut State University, VanderCook College of Music, Villanova University, and Duquesne University. Smaller satellite programs were initiated at Regis College, St. Mary's College (San Antonio),

Madonna University, The College of St. Catherine, Fontbonne College, Azusa Academy of Music in Glasgow, Scotland.

The goal was to develop meaningful and pragmatic courses for graduate credit where music educators could meet great teachers, conductors, composers and performers within the field of music and music education during the summer months.

This vision connected me with he greatest individuals in the field of music performance and music education. My talent was to network local music teachers with the music and music education gurus who wanted to help music teachers in the field who needed information, guidance, motivation, and materials to motivate themselves and their students in the classrooms of their local schools. The network of colleges and universities offered such opportunities for graduate credit and continuing education credit.

At present this network of graduate music education study attracts approximately 2,000 students each summer which represents approximately 1 million students in grades K-12. The reality of this vision which began in the summer of 1981 has to date inspired approximately 30,000 teachers representing approximately 15 million students.

With all this human energy, hard work, and commitment, only recently have I begun to understand the power of this spiritual calling. This calling was not for name recognition, political power, ego boosting, or financial gain. This calling was spiritual and designed to help the teachers help the children.

With this global effort of helping teachers and children, I have connected with an increased flow of love, caring, happiness, peace and joy which defines the mission of one's soul and allows one to know the purpose for which they are here and where they are going. Sharing these visions and insights of the past 30 years, I hope will help others open the doors to their spiritual calling, spiritual mission and spiritual purpose for being here at this time in the history of the universe.

I hope that by sharing my life-changing lessons learned from mentors and students spanning five decades others will be inspired to write about their unique journey of life-changing lessons. This is how we all connect from generation to generation, and those within our sphere of influence will be forever grateful.

Larry D. Allen

Larry D. Allen

ANYWAY

People are unreasonable, illogical, and self-centered,
LOVE THEM ANYWAY

If you do good, people will accuse you of selfish, ulterior motives,
DO GOOD ANYWAY

If you are successful, you will win false friends and true enemies,
SUCCEED ANYWAY

If you do good, it will be forgotten tomorrow,
DO GOOD ANYWAY

Honestly and frankness make you vulnerable,
BE HONEST AND FRANK ANYWAY

What you spent years building may be destroyed overnight,
BUILD ANYWAY

People really need help but may attack you if you help them,
HELP PEOPLE ANYWAY

Give the world the best you have and you'll get kicked in the teeth,
GIVE THE WORLD THE BEST YOU GOT ANYWAY

From a sign at Shishu Bhavan, the children's home in Calcutta

CHAPTER ONE

The Spiritual Call: Teach Children through Music

At age seven, I received the clearest of all angelic sounds - a sound which was a sign from God that we are going to perform a duet throughout my life towards a mission yet to be determined. This angelic sound as a sign from God manifested itself through my survival of a life-threatening illness that should have easily ended my life in 1954. The illness attacked my body with a cunning force - a ruptured appendix that did not appear on repeated blood tests. After seven days of non-stop excruciating abdominal pain and no ability to keep down any food, I found myself in the emergency room of St. Elizabeth Hospital in Dayton, Ohio unable to walk and gangrene pouring from a ruptured appendix towards my lungs.

Emergency surgery was ordered at 1:00 a.m., and I clearly remember that awful smell of ether as the mask was placed over my face. As I went to sleep, I remember that my dreams were racing, and I could recall and control my thoughts in any order while floating through the air and look back at myself on the operating table.

When I awoke, I discovered a huge bandage across my abdomen and four shots of penicillin daily. The food included goats milk and lots of vegetables with few things I enjoyed eating. After one week in the hospital I returned home. My first event at home was to pass ball with my dad in the backyard. It felt great. I knew at that moment that God had sent a strong message, a message that was calling me to do important work while on earth. The years ahead would be a journey to prepare myself to understand that important mission and carry it out.

In 1957 my family joined the white flight out of the Westwood District of Dayton, Ohio to a new small town north of Dayton called Englewood. Although I did not know it at the time, this move would establish the "home place" for my family for the next four decades. I was in the fifth grade and our new house was not completed by the beginning of the school year. Thus, my family drove me daily back and forth to school from our old home in Westwood for a number of weeks into the school year.

Early in the month of September my mother received a notice about a meeting for parents and students regarding the beginning band instrument program. I was most interested in music and listened to a great deal of music at home. However, the meeting was on my father's bowling night and mother just received her driver's license and had never driven at night. The meeting was scheduled for 7:00 p.m. in the school band room which was 10 miles from our old house in Westwood.

Much to her dismay, my mother drove me to the meeting, and I had the opportunity that evening to select a band instrument - the alto saxophone. This one evening changed my life forever and set me on a long and wonderful journey. Forty-two years later I now see that this move to Englewood, Ohio was no accident. It would give me an opportunity to begin the journey for which I was called. As we drove home from the meeting, I remember how nervous my mother was driving in the night traffic. Repeatedly cars from the other direction were driving with their high beams on at all times. After the first few cars my mother began talking to these drivers, then she became angry, and finally she retaliated by trying to shine her high beams at the oncoming drivers. The problem was that with every car that frustrated her she could not find the small foot switch that would trigger her high beams. After the 5th and 6th try I was laughing so hysterically that tears were streaming down my face. We talked about that night for years!

My mother was never big on driving, but on this one night her efforts to provide me an opportunity to play a band instrument was not by accident. It was clearly the most important night of my school years. This was all part of the spiritual journey. Fate, destiny, and energy in the universe far outweigh the wants and likes of individuals, groups, or large organizations. On this night I was to experience my first step towards a career in music education.

As I progressed in band on the saxophone, my first big break in music came in the summer between 7th and 8th grade. The high school band director, Dick Cool, needed additional players to complete his marching band instrumentation. Nine 8th graders were selected to travel to the high school daily for the band. This required a teacher to drive us and pick us up during the actual school day. Prior to the beginning of school we went to band camp and were accepted as members of the Northmont High School Marching Band. What an experience!

Although the drive during the regular school day took its toll on us all, we were able to perform on Friday evenings at the football games and on Saturdays for parades. I can remember how much more challenging the music was for all of us, and all music had to be memorized by the Thursday of each week. We performed 5 different half time shows each season and a grand finale. Our pre-game show was a big deal as was our post-game show. We had fun, we traveled, and improved our musicianship.

Progressing through high school (1961 - '65) I found myself involved in band, orchestra, choir and drama. Solo and Ensemble Contest as well as all the large group contests kept me more than busy, and I found myself immediately successful in all these musical events. As the four years of high school progressed, I created a big band that later was named, THE KINGSMEN and with a neighboring high school big band THE KNIGHTS OF RHYTHM. We performed at many of the high school dances and proms in the Dayton, Ohio area. Both groups had a good sound, were inexpensive, and looked good on stage. This opportunity was my most creative golden nugget.

As I completed my high school years I thought that there were many signs, signals and mentors pointing me towards music. Although I was an Eagle Scout and was a student leader in church, I felt my calling was teaching in the field of music. As a member of the National Honor Society and seeking a career in teaching, the Northmont Teachers Association awarded me with their annual scholarship.

My band director, Dick Cool, awarded me with the John Philip Sousa Award. In addition, I was the student conductor of the band during my senior year and at the same time, conductor of the adult choir at my church. These accomplishments were the most powerful and helped me choose music as my focus in college.

Within months I found myself on the campus of Baldwin-Wallace College and spending my life in the Conservatory of Music for the next four years (1965 - '69). I am not sure why I landed at this institution, but it had a great reputation for music and music education; thus, being there was exciting. However, I knew that there must be another purpose for me being in music at this institution.

As I was the first child in the family to enter college life, all experiences were new and at times trying; however, my parents were proud to have their son at the college level and in a career he enjoyed. I was very aware that my parents would have preferred me to be in another field that would attract more prestige and more money during my working years; however, I thought I could make a significant contribution to music and music education. My concern was doing well in whatever field I pursued. There were plenty of others seeking pre-med, math, science, business, and law, but music was unique, fulfilling, and challenging.

I was seeking new mentors at Baldwin-Wallace College and it took two years before the arrival of Frank Battisti and Galen Kral. For me, the arrival of both professors was the answer to many, many prayers. Both were dynamic, knew their stuff, and liked me. The energy that I felt from both of these professionals was at times overwhelming. Simply, I could not spend enough time with them, and I knew their appearance on the campus was part of my journey. After two years of searching for mentors, the arrival of these two professors was pure joy!

Playing alto saxophone in the wind ensemble and oboe/English horn in the orchestra, I found myself performing onstage with Aaron Copland, Vincent Persichetti, Warren Benson, Norman Dello Joio, Vincent Abotto, Siguard Rascher, Paul Creston and Donald Sinta. In the spring of my freshman year I participated as an oboist and English hornist in the performance of the famous ST. MATTHEW PASSION by J. S. Bach with the faculty and members of the Cleveland Orchestra.

As the orchestra closed with the final chord of the final chorale I remember feeling the presence of God within the silence that followed the final chord. This spiritual energy was followed by the angelic sound of applause I had ever heard. It took me over a week to recover from the impact of that spiritual experience. With this performance I knew my professional destiny was music, and that God and I had again touched spiritually.

With this experience I began to reflect through my past and determined that God and I had been performing a duet together on a long journey, and beginning with my near death experience at age 7, I was being directed on a spiritual journey. This was a journey that I was not controlling, but a journey that felt very natural. My destiny was yet to be realized, but with my participation in the performance of this great classical work by J.S. Bach, I felt comfortable that I was on the correct spiritual path.

Our music methods with Frank Battisti took place during the 1967-68 school year. Frank was outstanding in this class. There were twelve of us in the class and we were apostles for music education. Among many emotional events that year, the famous pianist from the Julliard School of Music in New York, Beveridge Webster, was scheduled months in advance to perform on campus in April, but no one could have projected that during the day of his evening concert scheduled on campus Martin Luther King, Jr. would be assassinated.

Although there was much upset about whether or not the concert should proceed, the decision was made to have the concert performed as scheduled. It was clear from the beginning that the artist was visibly upset, but he proceeded through the first composition by memory only to experience a memory lapse a few measures into the music.

He proceeded to perform the entire concert with music. This was a powerful sign for me and redefined the depth of character, the depth of spirituality, and the depth of caring necessary to be a classical music artist at this level of professionalism. I found myself bonding to this realization and knowing that from this spiritual depth I wanted to build my personal and professional life.

The culmination of my four years at Baldwin-Wallace College Conservatory of Music was my student teaching in the fall of 1968. I found myself working at at Strongsville High School on a daily basis working with the elementary, junior high and high school bands. It was a great experience in that the marching band was in full swing both at the high school and at the college. I was asked to complete a marching band arrangement of the current pop tune "Love is Blue" which was performed by both the Strongsville High School Marching Band and the Baldwin-Wallace College Marching Band.

As the semester progressed, the Baldwin-Wallace College Marching Band was invited to perform for the Buffalo Bills/San Diego Chargers football game on Sunday, November 17, 1968. We had worked hard for a number of weeks for this opportunity. On the day of the performance we boarded the buses for Buffalo and there was a light rain in the air; however, by the time we arrived in Buffalo the rain was so intense that the field was like soup with few yard line markers visible at any point on the field.

Our conductor, Frank Battisti and a few seniors examined the physical condition of the field which was simply unbelievable, and the quick decision was made to travel back to the campus. As a result, the prepared half-time show was never performed.

This was the biggest disappointment of my band experience at the college level. It took a long time to deal with this reality. I could rationalize that this was a test of my commitment and ability to put the hurt aside and go on with my journey in music. I have not had a similar challenge in music performance or music education, although over the years I have learned to take my mother's advice, "when life gives you lemons, make lemonade."

As I was going through the fall of 1968 and the ups and downs of the marching band season, I met a freshman who marched directly in front of me in the marching band. Little did I know this freshman, Judith Ann Kreeger, would become my soulmate. We dated for one year and were married on December 26, 1969. I immediately knew that this was the girl for me, and this is why my journey led me to Baldwin-Wallace College Conservatory of Music.

Judie was a most gifted bassoonist and clarinetist as she graduated from Nazareth Academy in Parma, Ohio and was on scholarship to the conservatory. This was the angels of angels and I knew immediately we were destined to be married and build a life together. This was God's doing and not mine. Our marriage would be God's will and I would go with the flow of God's energy and be grateful to know that my journey would now include a trio: God, Judie and myself. I completed my conservatory career by performing a senior oboe recital and performing as an English horn soloist with the wind ensemble. After four years I had performed all four passions of J. S. Bach and had successfully auditioned for a master's degree in oboe performance with Robert Bloom at the Hartt School in West Hartford, Connecticut. I was hired for a music teaching position in the East Harford, Connecticut Public Schools. The energy was flowing; the many signs along the pathway I had chosen were very clear, and the spiritual energy was very motivating.

As I made this transition from undergraduate student to a professional teacher and a masters student, I met many professional people from all walks of life who questioned my decision to follow a career in music. The major concern was money, prestige, and the return on the investment of time. Even during the graduation proceedings, the music education majors were seated in the back of the hall and the last to be called to the podium to receive their diplomas. I felt that this dynamic was a sign of how hard I would have to believe in my mission in life and the depth of the challenges I would have to confront to accomplish my spiritual mission in life.

I knew at age 22 that my journey would be challenging, but I knew God had given me the knowledge, stamina, and self-confidence to "weather the storms" ahead which I projected to be many in number. These "storms" would be life-changing experience, and I prepared myself to make things happen no matter what the obstacles or problems. My mission was to create new paradigms and new opportunities for children and families via music performance and music education. With this mission my goal was to unite people in all aspects of life worldwide. I was to be an international missionary with a mission of love and a talent who could bring people together at all levels of the spiritual and human condition.

My mission would include several dimensions: professional, personal, family, inter-personal and intra-personal. Keeping these dimensions in balance and in sequence would be the challenge; having the knowledge to be effective at all times would be the main thing, and having the spirit to know why all these dimensions were important would be paramount in understanding the reason for my journey and my contribution.

The 1969-70 school year would formally begin my mission. I had prepared 22 years for this first step. It was to begin in Connecticut with the base at the Hartt School in West Hartford, Connecticut.

CHAPTER TWO

The Parade of Angels: The Mentors

My earliest memory of needing mentors was in the third grade. I had survived a life-threatening attack that included a ruptured appendix in second grade and I knew that God had a plan for me. However, I was not sure what journey the plan would include and how I was not going to survive the journey physically, emotionally, or spiritually. My parents loved me very much and did all they could to nurture me. I felt as much love as any child on the planet, but I knew in third grade that I needed to reach out beyond my family.

The first step out of the family came on a sunny morning when I met my best friend, Phil Baker, at Westwood Lutheran Church. His mother taught Sunday school at the church and I was comfortable going to church knowing Phil and his mom would be there. I continued going to church and Sunday school alone for two years. I sang in the youth choir on Sunday and I have great memories of all the kids and adults associated with the church.

My best memory was my first Good Friday service and the sunrise Easter morning service. I remember all the black fabric draped over the statue of Jesus on Good Friday and how barren the church looked. I had never seen the church look like this and it was a little scary. On Easter morning I arrived at the church for the 6:00 a.m. sunrise service. There were trumpets, choirs, doughnuts, and many smiling faces. The church was filled with beautiful white flowers which I learned were Easter lilies. Everyone seemed different on Easter: happier and lighter in mood. It was terrific.

These two years at church were happy memories, I began reading stories from the Bible, made new friends and enjoyed singing in the children's choir. I remember that the church was newly constructed with two beautiful large church steeples made of brass; however, with each week the brass gradually turned green. I was never sure why this change in color was happening, but to a 10 year-old child the gradual change of the brass steeples from bronze to green looked awful.

However, my primary memory at this time in my life was the motivation to reach out on my own into the community. This gave me confidence as I knew that my journey and God's plan was going to have to include more great people like Phil Baker and his mom if I was to continue and fulfill God's plan.

We were living in Westwood which was on the west side of Dayton, Ohio. There was a tremendous energy of white flight to other outlaying communities in the late '50's and my family was caught up in this flight. I can still remember the day my parents announced that we were moving to the northern part of Montgomery County to the small town of Englewood. The town had less than 500 people, and I would begin a new life with new friends and hopefully a new church.

This move was immediately traumatic for me. Our new house was not completed before school started and I was looking for friends and mentors to help me in my new school. It seemed like we were traveling hours to and from school each day from our old house to my new school in our new neighborhood. The situation made it difficult to immediately make new friends and feel a part of the town. During the fall of 1957 Paul Anka had a hit tune, "Diana" and Jimmy Rogers also had a hit single "Honeycomb." I can remember listening to these hit singles over and over every morning as we drove to school and every afternoon returning back home.

I liked my 5th grade teacher, Mrs. Poince, and I was excited about starting the saxophone in the school band. private lessons were available on all instruments and my mom said that she would provide me the lessons. They were offered in the school day for $2.00 per 30 minutes.

Soon after we moved into our new house a call came from some very nice neighbors who asked me to be an acolyte for their new church. They knew I had attended a church of the same denomination in Westwood, and I was old enough to assist the new pastor at their new church that was meeting in my school cafeteria. The church was called Holy Trinity Lutheran Church. I was excited and knew that this was the first step of my journey in my new house and new town.

My first challenge was to set-up the church on Saturdays which was a weekly ritual from 1957-1961. At first, this was strange. I was going with adults to my school on Saturdays to change my school cafeteria into a church! For a ten-year-old this was new, different and took some adjustment. When we arrived on the first Saturday, the doors were opened which in itself seemed like we were doing something wrong even though I knew the church had permission. The first memory was walking into the cafeteria and smelling sour milk! That smell remained for all the years we used the church.

The drill was to take out all cafeteria tables, set the chairs in rows, bring out the piano and set-up the altar which was hidden on another floor. I would see the altar during school, but it was placed in a corner with its back facing out so that it looked like a large wooden box on wheels. Moving the altar up and down steps took at least 8 men plus us boys. There was a lot of groaning every move. A large white sheet was the backdrop which blocked the view of the kitchen, serving line and all the cafeteria carts and containers; however, it did not block that smell of sour milk!

Our first service was held in the gymnasium and was combined with another new church of the same denomination in a neighboring town. The churches were destined to separate and serve two different communities but for the first effort all families joined together and there I was going to church with Wayne & Sally Karlgaard and Ron & Shirley Parsons and their kids! This felt good to me. I met my new friends, and I was off to church for the first time not alone and at their invitation.

This was an answer to many prayers. My first challenge was to learn the liturgy and the role of the acolytes. I can remember being very excited and nervous on the first Sunday service. I dressed up for the first time with a long necktie. It was blue and square at the bottom. The material was different, but I did not know how to tie my own tie. I can remember needing help to tie that tie and for a few Sundays tying the blue necktie was "the" challenge.

As the church began with a wonderful pastor, Paul Winemiller, everyone knew that a permanent pastor would be arriving soon and all the families were very excited. I can still remember meeting our new pastor for the first time. His name was Wesley Runk and he was soon to become my first in a long string of mentors who would change my life forever.

This was a huge connection for me. I bonded instantly to Pastor Runk and we were like father and son for five years (fifth grade through ninth grade.) God has brought us together and I knew it. This was my main man, my main mentor and my inspiration.

I spent two years every Saturday in Catechism class where I and ten others learned all the books of the Bible and memorized biblical facts that would be part of our Confirmation. As my Confirmation date approached, my mentor families and Pastor Runk became friends with my parents and encouraged them to join the church and be baptized in the faith.

At this point I had been going to church alone for four years. What an experience to see my parents in church with me! On June 22, 1958 my one and only brother, Doug, was born. The timing was great! He was baptized, confirmed and eventually his children were baptized in the same church.

To this day Pastor Runk tells people about the young boy who brought his parents into the faith. The story has been repeatedly told by Reverend Runk to many congregations as one of his many unique stories of evangelism. For me, Confirmation went well, my parents became active in the church, and the church invested in property and built its own structure in 1961 just up the road from our house. Things were on a roll.

I clearly remember the ground breaking service outside, the laying of the cornerstone dated 1961 which contained the names of all the families in the church at that time, our first service inside, and a live nativity scene at Christmas. What great memories all these years later.

However, just as the church was moving its own with a new building and new families. I was notified by my mom that Pastor Runk was leaving the church to accept a similar position in a larger and more established church. I was crushed and not prepared to accept this reality, but part of me knew there was a reason for this separation. At fourteen years of age, I knew Pastor Wesley T. Runk was the model and mentor for me, and I knew that when he left there would be no other to replace his spot in my heart. My aspirations to be a member of the clergy, which was a serious consideration, came to an abrupt close with this experience and I knew from my journey in life was taking another direction with this dramatic loss in my life. With this sudden disappointment my soul knew that my journey beyond High School would not involve my mentor or a vocation as a pastor.

From 1962-1996 I did not have any contact with Pastor Runk; however, in February of 1996 my brother had a surprise for me and invited him and his wonderful wife, Marybeth, to our parents 50th Wedding Anniversary Surprise Party. It was a joy to see them both again. My parents were overwhelmed with the surprise and all those who showed their love by being a part of the festivities. As my father passed on two years later from prostate cancer, this event was one of the great memories of my parents' marriage of 50 years. They both felt the love of their friends and family over 50 years. It was a spiritual moment for me which I was able to capture on videotape.

Two years later I invited Pastor Runk to preside at the funeral service for my father which was held at Holy Trinity in Englewood, Ohio not knowing how he would feel about such an invitation. I was so pleased when he responded, "It would be an honor for me to do so."

Pastor Runk gave a beautiful eulogy of my dad and said that the main thing he remembered about my dad was his lack of interest in receiving public praise or credit for what he did for the church. That single perception of my dad was my connection to my own spiritual mission in life.

I knew I was to continue my spiritual mission and my spiritual journey where my dad had finished. This would include that single perception as my cornerstone for the future: No ego is necessary to achieve your spiritual goals as you teach children through music. This perception of my dad was powerful, true, and memorable; and I was open to hear it and know that my future would include this powerful vision for my own life.

~ WILLIS R. COOL ~

Everyone knew him as Dick Cool, band director of the Northmont High School Marching and Concert Bands in Clayton, Ohio. He gave his life to the program and to every student who had the good fortune to participate in the program. I was fortunate to be one of those students! His commitment was on one level very spiritual as he sacrificed many things in his life to provide himself and those who connected with him this wonderful music experience on a day to day basis that was at times almost hypnotic.

He worked and developed the Northmont High School Band program as if there was no clock, no time line, and no deadlines, just the joy of developing the program which ironically was very time consuming with many deadlines. I remember the long hours he would work with rehearsals, theory classes, contest deadlines, extra rehearsals and the many performances with marching band, concert band, and solo and ensemble contests. My high school years with the music program included 1961-'65.

Over the years many students went into the field of music and music education as both performers and teachers, and we all became addicted to his work ethic and commitment to the program. The dedication to the band program by Dick Cool was very, very contagious. There were no obstacles: physical, psychological or emotional that could disrupt his journey. There was a great deal of pride in this band and the program was building with our class - the first class to complete the new 7-12 consolidation of both the Randolph and Phillipsburg Schools into the new Northmont Schools.

My family moved to the Northmont School district two years before the consolidation of the Randolph and Phillipsburg Schools became a reality. The former Randolph Band program under the direction of Dick Cool received a big boost by this combination of schools into a much larger junior high and senior high school band program. Little did I know at the time that this coincidence of my family's move to Englewood, Ohio at the time of the consolidation of two school systems would be the single biggest factor determining my mission and my journey through life.

My earliest memories of Dick Cool and the Northmont High School Band Program was the marching band. Summer rehearsals during the day outside and at night inside included new music arranged by the band director. Everything was handwritten movie themes, television themes, classical themes and musicals. All were written for an eight minute halftime show and a short pre-game show that included the playing of the National Anthem.

A work week for Dick Cool included arriving to school by 7:00 a.m. with multiple bags and briefcases for each project and show he was trying to complete. He would write the shows, rehearse the band, prepare for night rehearsals and teach private lessons with his day ending at 9:00 p.m. Simply, the band room was always open, Saturdays included. As he wrote 5 different 8-minute half-time shows per season, he had little time for eating and sleeping.

Band camp was the first intense rehearsal experience for me. There was a rustic camp complete with cabins, lodge, swimming pool, covered picnic area and a flat open space the size of a football field. The girls lived on one side of the camp area and the boys on the other. There was no electricity and rustic toilet facilities. The camp was always the week before school: The last week of August which was followed by the local county fair performance over Labor Day. School began on the Tuesday after Labor Day.

The band performed five different shows per season (everything was memorized) and marched in a variety of parades. As a new school system building for the band program, there were many new and first-time experiences for the band during my four years in the program.

Band camp was where we learned the bulk of the drill, pre-game show and the music for the first show. Everything was memorized during this five day period. Some of the arrangements would not be completed until the day we rehearsed it! This required the conductor to spend long nights writing music and many hours at his thermo-fax machine, a rustic version of the present day photocopy machine. It was slow and it worked with a high-intensity heat lamp. I watched Dick consume many doughnuts in one bite to keep up with the timer that was on this machine. If your copy was under the lamp too long it would burn the print into the paper and your copy was all black.

The Northmont High School Band quickly became the pride of the local community. Ranking behind the basketball program and football program the band program was probably third in respectability as a competitive activity. In the early sixties sports were popular in high schools but not dominant in school life like they became in the mid-70's and beyond. Thus, band was one of the major competitive school activities. Sports for high school students in the 60's were very limited by the standards of comprehensive high school sports programs of the 1990's.

As I watched Dick Cool build the band and observed the community rally behind both he and the program, it was clear that Dick Cool was quickly becoming a local hero and all of us in the program were the proud recipients and benefactors of his hard work and dedication. The marching band began competing in newly created festivals and the concert band participated in the traditional contest formats. Both programs were excelling and increasing in their awards, accomplishments and reputation.

During marching season, the band had one dress rehearsal every Thursday evening before the Friday night football game. The rehearsal was under the lights at the home field and all band students were required to have the new half-time show memorized by that time. The football team always took the field at 6:00 p.m. followed by the band at 7:30. Each section of the band met at the field at 6:30 where everyone had to play their music by memory for their respective section leaders. The section leaders reported the results to the band director before practice began.

These Thursday night rehearsals were very important to the band and they took place in almost all types of weather. I can remember more than one evening when the band rehearsed with Dick Cool physically very ill. He was once so ill that he could not talk, but he would show up and rehearse the band anyway. He approached the band no differently than all the great football coaches. He wanted perfection and he wanted to win. He was a great psychologist and we all needed what he was providing us and the program at that time of life: self-esteem as individuals and as a group.

One Thursday evening after the rehearsal we were loading the famous "band truck", a 1953 Chevrolet with wooden side rails. There were a handful of us who would load and unload this truck every Thursday as the football field was five miles away from the high school.

Largely, we hauled the percussion instruments and large brass instruments; however, for one show the art department built wooden spears out of long pieces of wood with cardboard points on the end sprayed in bright gold. We loaded these artistic spears onto the truck with the other traditional gear.

As we drove off, I noticed that one by one the spears were falling off the truck onto the road. It was 9:30 p.m. and difficult to see. We turned around and began to retrace our direction picking up the spears as we went. Suddenly, an oncoming car lost control and came over into the path of the band truck. We were moving slowly, but the driver saw it was us and immediately swerved to the left to avoid hitting us head-on. The driver of the car was a parent and a strong band supporter. He was not hurt in the accident, but it could have been more serious if we would have hit head-on.

Concert Band Contest in Ohio is a tradition! Our band was at the state band competition in Columbus, Ohio. Our band had worked hard and had done well at the regional contest; thus earning the opportunity to progress to the state level of competition.

We arrived early to the contest site and heard other bands perform. After lunch we went through our regular warm-up drills, tuned and progressed to the stage. Our performance went well as did our sight reading, but there were a few rough moments that were of concern. When they posted our scores we barely achieved a level I rating of superior performance, but we clearly met our goal for this performance.

We were all excited with some calling home, others calling the local radio station and other in the euphoria of the moment. We all boarded our buses for home and waited for the traditional pep talk from our band director before leaving for home. However, when Dick Cool boarded the bus, his pep talk was cut short. One of his student assistants had incorrectly read the judges comment sheet and we just missed the superior level I rating. We received a level II rating.

The group was devastated and never emotionally recovered through the balance of the year. I perceived this event as a devastating disappointment at the time and understood this experience to be another sign of directing me in my journey ahead.

My mission in life was still a mystery to me, but I knew that there were going to be very clear signs to point me in the right direction that would appear as repeated blocks and obstacles. From these upsets and disappointments I was to learn of my mission and my direction.

Watching the response of the band from this competitive experience soured me on the need for large group competition as part of a school music program. Individual solo or concerto competition or chamber music competitions sounded more appropriate to me.

In later years I would return to visit Dick Cool and ask him why he was so dependent on the contest format to complete a season with he band. He responded, "It is the only format where I can motivate the students to perform at their highest level of ability." I was disappointment with his response but knew that in his situation he was correct and very honest in his reasoning.

After Dick Cool retired from Northmont High School, he began working in the field of music technology. I was pleased to include Dick and his team in our Summer Music Institutes at central Connecticut State University. It was a joy to be able to support him and give him an opportunity to teach at the graduate level in his retirement days.

The next step in my journey would be a music conservatory. Dick recommended Baldwin-Wallace College Conservatory of Music and that was where I landed for four years of music training. During the 1964-65 school year the Baldwin-Wallace College Wind Ensemble premiered two new marches by John Cacavas: "Days of Glory" and "LaBella Roma."

Dick invited me to guest conduct the pieces on the spring concert of my senior year. It was difficult to say "good-bye" to Dick Cool and Northmont High School in 1965, but my journey was continuing and I knew I would need to find new mentors at Baldwin-Wallace College to help me stay on course.

~ ROGER DECKER ~

Private music teachers are a special breed of teacher. They do all the important skill work with individual students but receive very little public acclaim. These teachers are the reason students develop into outstanding professional musicians. Roger Decker was my first private lesson teacher on the alto saxophone. He was outstanding. He performed professionally on flute, clarinet and alto saxophone while I studied with him at Suttmiller's Dinner Theater in Dayton, Ohio.

Roger was fun, talented, energetic and was an outdoor person with a canoe anchored on top of his little two-door import car. Our lessons were held in the janitor's storage room between the barrels of soap concentrate, cleaning fluids, mops, brushes and other cleaning material.

My lessons began in the 5th grade on Thursday mornings at 10:00. The school supported the release of the students for music lessons providing the student was doing well academically. Lessons were $2.00 per half hour in 1957. I took lessons in the fall, spring and summer with Roger. I studied weekly with him for 5 years which is the longest period of time I ever studied with any individual in any subject.

I still attribute my success in music to the lessons I had with him. His expertise included tone and rhythm, and he could sight-read almost any piece of music with little difficulty. One of my greatest memories of Roger was going to Suttmillers Dinner Theater and listening to him and the band perform throughout the evening. I was so proud to be his student.

Roger was into so many things other than music and it was interesting just to be with him. Similar to the Wesley Runk experience, I was notified one day that Roger was moving to Orlando, Florida where there were more opportunities for him to perform in a new Disney complex that was being built there.

This was another wonderful mentor whom I knew could never be replaced. My disappointment was again at an all-time high, and I did not have an opportunity to say "good-bye" to him. The memories were deep and sweet, but again, I knew there would be no other Roger Decker in my life.

One of my fantasies was to travel to Orlando and just call him on the phone or visit him. In 1992 I was on a business trip and changed planes in Orlando. While waiting at the airport, I looked through the local phone book to find Roger Decker. At first I thought I would not be able to find him, but sure enough, there his name was: three Roger Deckers in the book.

I dialed the first one and, immediately, I recognized not just the voice but the rhythm of his words. After six years of weekly lessons, one just knows the voice after all these years, and he was not going to remember me.

I simply said, "Roger, this is Larry Allen. I was one of your former saxophone students at Northmont. Do you remember me?" What do I do if he says, "I do not remember you" or "Sorry, you have the wrong Roger Decker." I was so prepared to hear some version of these two answers that I almost missed his reply which was, "Larry, of course I remember you." He proceeded to list all the students who studied with him at Northmont and wanted to know how everyone was doing. I had waited 30 years for that one moment. Roger sounded great, he was feeling great and he was very interested in what I was doing.

Roger Decker help many students, was extremely gifted and had a tremendous passion for music. That he remembered me was enough. I expressed my caring, love and appreciation for all he had done for me and that my future was a result of many of the things he had taught me about music and life.

I wondered how many of his students went on to a music conservatory, graduated and developed a career in music performance and/or music education. Roger was a spiritual mentor and we connected at the highest level. The most appropriate "thank-you" I can give Roger for all he did for me is to keep his spirit alive by my caring, love, appreciation and willingness to do for others what he did for me.

~ BILL HARROD ~

Wanting to expand my musical experience to the orchestra, I began the oboe in the summer before my 10th grade year in high school at the invitation of my band director. My first oboe teacher was Bill Harrod, oboist with the Cincinnati Symphony Orchestra. Bill was a tremendous artist as both an oboist and English hornist. I remember the first time I heard him perform in concert. I was so impressed with his talent and proud to be his student.

Lessons were on Saturdays at Roetter Music in Dayton, Ohio. I rode the public bus transportation 20 miles round trip for my weekly oboe lesson. I was amazed at how much more difficult it was to obtain a pleasing sound on the oboe as compared to the alto saxophone which I had been playing since 5th grade. The sequential years of playing both saxophone and oboe gave me an appreciation of what my future oboe students would be going through and struggling with as beginners.

Listening to Bill play the oboe with such sweet vibrato was like magic to a beginner, and I was both surprised and overwhelmed at the time at how accurately he could sing the beautiful melodic lines written for the oboe. Working closely with a professional performer on a weekly basis was the catalyst for moving my musical interests into the orchestral world. I have Bill Harrod to thank for his inspiration, teaching and modeling. With this motivating experience, I knew that being a good music teacher must include being an outstanding performer.

~JACK BOWSHER ~
~ KEN WHITE ~

In addition to my religious and musical mentors, here were two leaders in our local Boy Scout Troop 356. Although there were a number of scout leaders that were inspirational and had good leadership skills, both Jack Bowsher and Ken White were a great team who cared deeply about their own sons in scouting but reached out to others like myself and gave us all the time, energy and skills to enjoy the many scouting challenges.

I was fortunate to have leaders that encouraged me to achieve scouting's highest award, "Eagle Scout" and the highest religious award, "Pro Deo Et Patria". I felt that scouting gave me many leadership opportunities, travel experiences and unique challenges that extended far beyond church and school.

I always felt that a scouting experience for all youth was directly proportional to the quality and dedication of the parent leaders. The numerous merit badges that required parent direction, driving, weekend camp-outs, week-long camp-outs, camporees, jamborees and unique projects that included marksmanship and building small hydroplanes are examples of the hard work and commitment that both Jack Bowsher and Ken White devoted to us all.

Personally, I know that all I learned in scouting and all I achieved in scouting I owe primarily to these two gentlemen, and I will be forever grateful for being there for me and others in the troop.

~ FRANK L. BATTISTI ~

Many knew him as Mr. B, but to me he was the sign I had been looking for over a two-year period of time. Frank L. Battisti arrived on the campus of Baldwin-Wallace College Conservatory of Music in November of 1967 and my whole life changed with this single event.

As President of the local chapter of Kappa Kappa Psi (the band fraternity,) I was responsible for helping with the connections and arrangements for meeting Frank. Our first meeting included dinner with he and a number of fraternity members.

The fraternity paid for the meal and whatever arrangements were appropriate for this first meeting. This first meeting experience was magical! Everyone was very excited and motivated about Frank's past, his successes in band conducting and the many premieres of new music for the band that he had conducted which earned him a reputation of being at the "forefront of band literature."

The list of outstanding musicians that came to the campus because Frank was there was most impressive and musically inspiring. The tours and special events he organized for the group were first-time experiences for most of us in the group. My role was to keep the students and our new conductor connected and on the same track. Whatever I could do to make this transition time work for everyone was my single agenda.

I had never seen a professional work so hard and be so dedicated to a discipline as Frank was to quality band performance and music education. He was a mentor's mentor, a conductor's conductor and a friend's friend. There were no limits with Frank. He was interested in dedication, beauty, perfection and wonderful music-making. I often felt that I would never be able to measure up to his stamina and dedication, and most of his students felt the same.

During my two years with Frank, I experienced a loyalty and friendship that's was unique and spiritual. Between November, 1967 and June, 1969, the country went through some amazing experiences. For most of these experiences, I had the opportunity to share them with Frank as did others. His insights, his philosophy and his motivation gave me a new dimension as to what my mission would be in life and how I would attempt to achieve my goals. If ever there were a listing of gurus fro bands in America, Frank would be on the top of the list. The experience could be labeled as pure joy and happiness at all times. The coincidence of Frank choosing Baldwin-Wallace College at the same time I was there was no accident. Frank was the mentor I had been looking for for over two years. I felt renewed and back on track with my life and my mission.

~ GALAN KRAL ~

During the 1967-68 school year, Galan Kral arrived at Baldwin-Wallace Conservatory of Music with his wife, Inge, as the new professor of oboe and saxophone. He had just finished twenty years with the Baltimore Symphony Orchestra. He was an outstanding teacher and dedicated to the art of teaching oboe among other aspects of music. He successfully transformed all the oboists and their respective sounds with work on embouchure, reed-making and breathing techniques.

One of the high points in my two years with Galan was the annual performances of the Bach Festivals which included both faculty and student performers. In hindsight, this annual opportunity was heaven on earth. I can remember how much we all admired Galan, helped him and his wife, Inge, move into their home and the close friendship we maintained in the years after we graduated.

As I moved on to study with Bert Lucarelli and Robert Bloom, I can still hear Galan tell me how I would soon forget him as I progressed in my musical life. I promised him that I would never let that happen, and I kept my promise.

Galan Kral arriving to the campus was also coincidence. he was there to help us all, but he was preparing me for my next step in life. I knew then that whatever was in my future was in the hands of Galan, and his zest for being an outstanding teacher was the example I needed to know, feel and model. His knowledge and skills were second to none, but his insights into people and situations were even more brilliant than his musical and teaching skills. I admired his modesty, self-confidence and inner strength. This was the man who was going to help me launch my future as an oboe performer and oboe teacher. I thank him for inspiring me to inspire hundreds of private oboe students over the past thirty years.

My prayer is that all teachers can find a '"Galan Kral" in their years of training at the university level. It is my feeling that many hope for such experience, with a mentor and those who are seeking it actually find this type of opportunity.

~ ROBERT BLOOM ~
~ HUMBERT LUCARELLI ~

The late Robert Bloom is considered by most oboists to be one of the icons of the oboe world in the 20th century. He was a great man, a tremendous musician and a wonderful performer. His life and his teaching touched the lives of thousands of students, professional musicians and audiences. It was my good fortune to audition for him, be accepted to do my Masters degree at the Hartt School of Music with him over two years (196901971.) Again, this coincidence was not by accident.

This opportunity to study for two years with Robert Bloom was my biggest accomplishment to date. I was on the campus on two weeks when I met an older student of Robert Bloom: Bert Lucarelli! The combination of these two geniuses of the oboe would change my life again, forever. Both these oboists had different styles of oboe performances, but we bonded in their love of the oboe and their dedication to advance the instrument during their lifetimes.

In October of 1969 Bert Lucarelli presented the first concert in Alice Tully Hall in New York City. It was the first of a series of outstanding recitals and concerts by Bert in New York. His career as '"America's Leading Oboe Soloist" was launched and all of his students (including myself) were there to witness a new, exciting paradigm in oboe history: developing a career as an oboe soloist rather than a career as a symphony musician.

Both Robert Bloom and Bert Lucarelli were "'pied pipers", great performers and great teachers. They both became legends in their own time in the world of oboe performance and oboe teaching. Both represented two different generations of oboe performance and teaching. My greatest memory was watching them both perform in duet on the stage at Alice Tully Hall with the Bach Aria Group.

One of the greatest stories that was told to me by Bert regarding Robert Bloom was his frustration in not being able to match the sound of Robert Bloom. Finally, one day he confessed to his mentor that he could not match his sound and perform the oboe with his style. Mr. Bloom responded, "Bert, I never expected you to perform as a clone of anyone else. I expect you to perform like Bert Lucarelli."

With that statement Bert Lucarelli became "America's Leading Oboe Soloist." His contributions tohis flock of students worldwide have been unmeasurable. As one member of his flock, I knew then as I know now that my opportunity to spend two years with him as his student was not by accident. This was a destiny for me that was well charted before our paths crossed as teacher and student.

There are many professional oboists worldwide who continue to make wonderful contributions to the field of oboe performance, teaching and literature; however, to be able to work simultaneous as part of one's Master Degree in oboe performance with Robert Bloom and Bert Lucarelli was a major life-changing experience. Students of both these icons can only hope to pass on to the next generation their inspiration and dedication to the oboe. I am most humbled and grateful for the opportunity to have studied with them both.

~JACK ALEXANDER ~

During the 1970-71 school year, I was hired by the West Hartford Public Schools to teach music. Jack Alexander was the person who made this possible. He was the director of music town wide in grades K-12, and he was looking to make things happen in music education at all grade levels. I worked daily from 1970-1976 at Talcott Junior High School (grades 7-9) while performing with the Hartford Symphony Orchestra and completing my Masters Degree at the Hartt School of Music.

Innovation was the motivation during my teaching in West Hartford with many opportunities to create national models of excellence at the junior high level in music curriculum, electronic music and interdisciplinary programs with music and other academic disciplines. Jack Alexander was there for me and opened the door for these ideas and programs at Talcott Junior High School to become national models for all schools throughout the balance of the 20th century.

Immediately I found myself at state, regional and national music conventions outlining our program at Talcott Junior High School. The students in electronic music were producing their own recordings and having the recordings performed in prime time on the local rock station with students being interviewed in the music classroom from the rock radio station. This was a great experience for 14 year-old students who were not in the band, orchestra or choir programs.

All of this national attention and innovation was made possible by the administrative support of Jack Alexander. Little did I know at the time that the Assistant Superintendent of Schools for instruction, Ira, Singer, would be observing my work and launch me to the next turn in the road of my journey.

~ IRA SINGER ~

During my years in the West Hartford Public Schools, Dr. Ira Singer was both loved and respected by all who knew him and by all who worked with him professionally. He was a man of great vision and had a love of the arts. During the 1976-77 school year he took a new position in the Pittsfield Massachusetts Public Schools as Superintendent of Schools.

One of the two high schools, Taconic High School, was expanding its total schedule to a seven-period for the first time ever. As such, there was room for music and the development of a band program. Dr. Singer asked me to apply and eventually I became the school's first band director seven years after the school was built. I signed my contract assuming that my wife would sign the contract she was offered in music therapy, but at the last minute there was an unavoidable conflict and she could not accept the position in Pittsfield. Living in Southington, Connecticut, I found myself commuting 90 miles each way to school for one year.

Beginning a new program at the high school level involved an interesting sequence of recruiting students via phone who had not performed on their instrument since junior high school. It was my hope that this network of students still had the instruments in the attic and would be interested in bringing them out of the attic and resume their musical experience. As the year progressed, we produced two recordings, traveled to Westmount High School in Montreal in an exchange program, developed an electronic music lab, initiated the first marching band, developed a chamber music series and in general surprised ourselves as to how much we could do together. One of our seniors went to the University of Massachusetts to complete degrees in music education and conducting.

As the year progressed, I found myself flying to school daily from Brainard Field in Hartford, Connecticut to the Pittsfield airport. A colleague from West Hartford, Bill Deegan, also took a position in Pittsfield in the area of television production. He was a pilot, had an airplane that seated two and was interested in teaming with me in the daily commute. it was interesting flying to school daily during the first grading period!

However, as the weather became more inclement, we found ourselves commuting via car, and eventually, Bill and his family purchased a home in Pittsfield and I found myself commuting the balance of the year alone via a car. This teaching opportunity was a great experience, but Dr. Singer knew I could not continue to commute daily for a career.

As such, it was mutually agreed that I should try for a position closer to home! With this high school experience and all the innovation I interviewed for my next opportunity: my first full-time administrative position. As the summer approached in 1977, I was invited to interview for the K-12 Director of Music position in the Glastonbury, Connecticut Public Schools.

On July 11, 1977 I was selected to begin this position as of August 1. My new boss would be Henry

Schoebel. I felt that all my hard work over the past 8 years had paid off! I now was working as an administrator in one of the leading school systems in Connecticut. This opportunity was a major turn in the road on my journey. This part of my journey would last ten years.

~ HENRY SCHOEBEL ~

Henry Schoebel was the Assistant Superintendent of the Glastonbury Public Schools in 1977, eventually he became Superintendent of Schools and retired all within my 10-year tenure there (1977-1987.) These ten years of creativity and innovation were the zenith of my first twenty years in music education. The school system wanted me to bring energy, creativity and innovation to the K-12 music curriculum which needed a boost.

Hiring new teachers and retiring old ones was the biggest challenge over 10 years while at the same time creating new programs at the elementary, junior high and high school levels. The list innovations included an Inter-Elementary Music Festival, Summer Music and Art Program, Electronic Music Programs, Inter-Disciplinary Program with music, science and foreign languages, The Artist-in-Residence Program with Dr. Moshe Paranov, The Connecticut Band and Orchestra Symposium and the Symphony at Salmon Brook with the Hartford Symphony Orchestra performing with our high school band, orchestra and choir, and the Fall Workshops for Music Educators.

With all these opportunities and creations I was in my element and the school system was encouraging me and others to continue our energy and efforts. I was not sure how all of this was going to progress or if I was to complete my life as a music educator in Glastonbury; however, with such an outstanding staff of teachers and the encouragement of the administration, I was establishing national models of excellence and I knew I was in the right place at the right time of my life.

~ MOSHE PARANOV ~

Among our listing of innovations included the celebrated ARTIST-IN-RESIDENCE PROGRAM featuring Dr. Moshe Paranov, President Emeritus of the Hartt School of Music. Dr. Paranov began working with us in the Glastonbury Public Schools in 1979 at 86 years of age! He continued to develop the program in Glastonbury and because of the program's immediate success, Dr. Paranov branched out to other area schools bringing outstanding talents with him from the Hartt School of Music.
My work with Dr. Paranov continued for 10 years. At age 96 he was still lecturing, performing at the piano and bringing outstanding programs for audiences of all ages.

The listing in-school concerts and community concerts were endless! Wherever possible Dr. Paranov combined the students with the professionals at all age levels. Soloists, chamber music and large ensembles were included in the programs as well as interdisciplinary programs combining music with foreign languages, physics and English.

Having retired officially from the Hartt School of music in1970 at age of 75, Dr. Paranov had still retained his zest for beautiful music and wanted to continue to find ways to being great music into the lives of school teachers, administrators, students and parents. He had the ability and talent throughout his life to ignite a fire in his audiences and in his performers on-stage.

Performances under his direction were magical and he won the respect of all who worked with him. From 1979-1989, my life was changed forever through constant contact and teaming with Dr. Paranov. The lessons of life, music and teaching were truly angelic sounds that I was destined to hear about and to know. I knew that I would never again have such an opportunity to work in a relationship like I experienced with Dr. Paranov; thus, everyday was special. A few of his many quotations are memorable:

"When you know you do not know, then you know."

"I love working with young people between the ages of 15 - 25 because they know everything. There is never a reason to worry."

"When I began teaching in my twenties, I thought I knew everything. When I was in my thirties, I started to become restless. At forty I was nervous. At fifty I was unsure of myself. At sixty I started to panic. At seventy I knew I needed help. At eighty I was exhausted. Finally, at ninety I began to know a little something about life."

The opportunity for me to know Dr. Paranov was a coincidence that was destined to occur. I was glad I knew without a question while working with him that God had brought us together during a time in both our lives where we needed each other. My genuine appreciation of all he and his wife, Libby Warner-Paranov, did for me can only be expressed by what I am doing for others in my life using their example of love and caring.

In 1983 the famous report, A NATION AT RISK, was published and many educators felt compelled to expand the course curriculum at the high school level, to increase graduation requirements and consider more intensity in the area of academics.

Our response in Glastonbury included developing a new community outreach by bringing into the community the major symphony orchestra of the region, The Hartford Symphony Orchestra, and included the high school band, orchestra and choir performing with the H.S.O.; plus awarding a $1,000.00 scholarship for the winner of the concerto competition. To make this plan work we needed the support of the local business community. John Hamby, President of Glastonbury Band and Trust stepped up and took a leadership role. He raised $25,000.00 and the event took place with great fanfare and community support. The format expanded to the towns of Simsbury and Southington in the years ahead and this new community outreach connected professional musicians with school music students and local communities.

The format could never have begun without the vision and support of John Hamby who always reminded me that the 1980's was an era of self-enlightenment, and as such, we needed to demonstrate to the area businesses what they would receive in return for their investment in our new program which was entitled: THE SYMPHONY AT SALMON BROOK CORPORATE PARK.

Having a school music director working with the area businesses and corporations was unprecedented and in many local communities this type of working relationship would be viewed as awkward; however, John Hamby saw that the more we could integrate the community with the school students and the professional musicians, the better the outcome would be. He was correct on all counts and the rest is history.

John Hamby was the single individual who could make this effort work for the community. I knew at the time that without his vision and caring the project would simply be an idea whose time had not yet arrived; however, it was a terrific coincidence to team with him and bring such a great idea for all to enjoy.

As the years progressed in the Glastonbury Public Schools, the innovation that became the "jewel in the crown" was the Fall Workshops for Music Educators which caught the attention of the Hartt School of Music. The series attracted the top leaders in music education to Glastonbury for our series of Wednesday workshops. It was Henry Schoebel who had organized the administration with a strong "curriculum director" format and was responsible for closing down school at 1:30 p.m. each Wednesday for professional staff development! Between 1976 and 1980, we were able to attract nationally-recognized music educators to Galstonbury and we would invite teachers from throughout the state to join us. All of this was paid for by Glastonbury Public Schools.

Working in Glastonbury, meeting Henry Schoebel and developing a workshop program that could exist on Wednesday afternoons due to administrative structure designed by Mr. Schoebel was my destiny. This opportunity would eventually lead to a new cottage industry in America: summer graduate courses for music educators.

I will forever be grateful to Henry Schoebel and the many Glastonbury opportunities. This directed me to my biggest accomplishment in the field; helping teachers help the students. For every teacher I could help, I could help on average 500 students worldwide. As I knew in 1981that this would be my biggest contribution in education, I was prepared to go the distance and take necessary risks as this opportunity unfolded.

~ DONALD HARRIS ~

In the summer of 1981 Donald Harris, the Dean of Hartt School of Music, invited me to adapt the Glastonbury Workshops for Music Educators for graduate credit for their annual summer program: SUMMERTERM '81 - WORKSHOPS FOR MUSIC EDUCATORS. I knew that this invitation could lead to a new paradigm for many in the field of music education and that millions of children over the years would benefit by bringing together interested teachers, pragmatic topics in K-12 music education and the world-class leaders who were expert on the many topics within the field of K-12 music education.

This innovation offered one-week courses in the summer and the Hartt School of Music advertised the program nationwide for the first time during the 1980-81 school year. I was given the position of director of the program and as my contract in Glastonbury was from September through June, I was able to direct this program during the summer months.

I had anticipated that music schools across the country would immediately imitate this program; however, only one school followed that expectation. In the summer of 1982, VanderCook College of Music in Chicago developed a summer program that duplicated the format of the Hartt School of Music. Little did I know in 1982 that my future would land at this institution to expand the school's vision nationwide in 1989.

This summer music program for music teachers was extremely successful as it continued to develop topics for graduate credit that were relevant to the needs of music educators worldwide, and there were outstanding leaders in music education that were complimented to be asked to teach summer one-week courses.

This launch of a new idea was critically important for many teachers worldwide. Donald Harris deserves the credit for making this possible for the entire industry. His vision and determination to reach out to music educators has my heartfelt respect and appreciation.

~ GLEN CHANDLER ~

In 1984 there was an interest by Central Connecticut State University to expand the format at the Hartt School of Music by offering more music educations courses and including other topics beyond what was currently being offered. Both of these programs in Connecticut continued to be the national models of excellence in the 1980's along with our colleagues at the VanderCook College of Music.

The key to this second step of the outreach at C.C.S.U. was the leadership of Dr. B. Glenn Chandler, chairman of the Department of Music. He embraced the idea of a summer program and worked closely with the President of the University who was very complimentary about this program and the music department's interest in initiating a national outreach.

The program was successful in its first year and quickly became the third national model of excellence of summer graduate study in music education following both the Hartt School and the VanderCook summer music programs.

Between 1984 and 1989 the programs on these three campuses blazed the trail for the next step: A national outreach on multiple campuses under one central administration. This effort was going to be initiated on one of these three campuses at some point. My destiny was to follow that reality wherever it would take me. I was soon to discover that VanderCook College of Music in Chicago would show the first interest in this national outreach effort. Glenn Chandler was a key person in the development of this outreach for teachers. Without his leadership and commitment the second step of this initiative could not have happened. I will always think of Glenn Chandler as a spiritual leader in music education and music scholar. We were an excellent team and I sincerely value his friendship, his spirit and his leadership.

~JIM GILWORTH ~

In the summer of 1998 Jim Gilworth, President of VanderCook College of Music asked if some of our clinicians at Central Connecticut State University could visit VanderCook College of Music and serve as clinicians during the summer of 1988. We agreed to share our clinicians and my first connection to VanderCook College of Music and Jim Gilworth began.

By the summer of 1989, I found myself working at VanderCook College of Music in Chicago and moving my family to the town of Valparaiso, Indiana. My mission was to develop a nationwide summer program for music directors under the sponsorship of VanderCook College of Music.

I was to develop the title of the program, sights, budget, course titles and clinicians. The program title was to be MECA (Music Education Centers of America) and the initial sites were to include Villanova University, Madona University, Fontbonne College, Regis College, St. Mary's University and The College of St. Catherine. The Villanova University site in Philadelphia quickly became the "jewel in the crown" in the 1990's, attracting nearly 1,000 registrations during the summer months.

~ MICHAEL KUMER ~

Unfortunately, there was an administrative turnover between the commitment of the MECA program and its development. Fortunately, one individual in the pool of clinicians was Michael Kumer, Dean of the School of Music at Duquesne University in Pittsburgh. he was interested continuing the national outreach energy of the summer music educators' program at Duquesne University. As a result, commitment was made in the summer of 1990 to develop the national outreach under the name SUMMER MUSIC INSTITUTES as a two-year outreach program.

Sites expanded from Azusa Pacific University to the Royal Scottish Academy of Music in Glasgow, Scotland as Duquesne University was interested in expanding its name and reputation. While all this developed, my family remained in Valparaiso, Indiana. I was commuting to Pittsburgh for meetings and staying in touch daily with Duquesne University via computer and FAX communication. I knew that at the end of the two-year project I would be asked to move to Pittsburgh and again, uproot my family.

In 1991 I was asked to make a decision to come to Pittsburgh as the Assistant Dean of the School of Music and continue as Director of the Summer Music Institutes. This was a wonderful opportunity for me, but I knew my family had to come first and I declined the invitation. As a result, I chose to remain in Valparaiso, Indiana and continue my journey. In August of 1992 I completed my professional relationship with Duquesne University.

Michael Kumer was the angel of angels and his vision, his commitment and his caring for Duquesne University and for the music educator community worldwide was a commitment the music education community had never witnessed. Dean Kumer will always receive my highest respect for his dedication and leadership between 1990 and 1992. It was a national model of excellence that has yet to be matched by another college or university. Duquesne University continues to sponsor SUMMER MUSIC INSTITUTES on an annual basis.

~ WILLIAM EIFRIG ~

As I moved to Valparaiso, Indiana to begin the new MECA program at VanderCook College of Music, I was interested in teaching oboe locally. Valparaiso University needed an oboe teacher and had a need for some innovation in music education. I met with William Eifrig, chair of the Department of Music, in April of 1989 and indicated that while I was developing the national outreach via VanderCook

College of Music, I would be interested in developing a studio at Valparaiso University.

At the same time, Dr. Eifrig invited me to establish a new non-credit outreach program for private music lessons. It became known as PARTNERS FOR MUSIC and was launched in the fall semester of 1990. This new program was good for all involved. Teachers received an increase in pay, the university received their portion for administration and taxes and the students experienced a high professional level of teaching on most band orchestra instruments, piano and voice.

I continued to provide a studio of oboe instruction at Valparaiso University for eleven years and the PARTNERS FOR MUSIC PROGRAM is beginning its 11th year of operation on campus. Dr. Eifrig was innovative and visionary in his concern for programs that reached beyond the traditional undergraduate curriculum. The coincidence of our teaming together to provide a new long range program was an important part of my journey.

~JIM RUBISH ~

In January of 1993 I received a call from La Porte Community Schools that there was an emergency and a music teacher was needed at Kesling Middle School. Students had been without a band director for a number of weeks and the administration was looking for someone who could step in and continue the program which already had performance deadlines on the calendar. I interviewed for the position, indicated I would be able to step in immediately, and the administration was interested in implementing the comprehensive curriculum I had built in West Hartford, Connecticut for both of their middle schools.

Within two days I found myself conducting the school jazz band not knowing anyone's name or background in music. The student were talented and were disappointed with the musical disruption of the school year. As the year progressed, the jazz band did a recording in Chicago as a tribute to their efforts and produced cassette tapes for participating students and their families. This was a special experience for me and I credit Jim Rubish, Principal of Kesling Middle School during this transaction who stepped in to help make the transition smooth and meaningful for the students.

I continued to teach 300 students at Kesling Middle School, including four levels of band and two levels of percussion and guitar classes in our Exploratory Music Program (for students not choosing band, orchestra or choir.) The Kesling Middle School students were a daily source of inspiration. I enjoyed the contrast of the students in the school and the rainbow of ideas, insights and inspiration the students brought to each class.

Over the years at Kesling, I learned to hear those angelic voices of the students in each class on a daily basis. These students changed my life and my priorities! My personal journey to Kesling was not an accidental coincidence. This teaching experience was designed to help me better help the students at the highest level of teaching and learning. In response, the students directed me to a higher spiritual experience by just doing and just being themselves. I have a grandmother and an aunt buried in Pine Lake Cemetery in La Porte, Indiana. I often wonder if their spiritual energy led me to La Porte, Indiana. I visit their graves and think of this spiritual connection.

~ ED SUETA ~

As I worked with a large volume of clinicians, experts and leaders in the field of music education, I was highly impressed with the work of Ed Sueta. He had worked hard in his musical life in New York City as a woodwind performer with terrific skills and insights in music and a special talent on flute and clarinet. I was first aware of his band method in the early 70's as a new band director, but little did I know how much influence he would have in my life.

As the SUMMER MUSIC INSTITUTES progressed, I became very aware of the strong impact Ed Sueta was having on band directors and the music education community at-large. He expanded his band methods in the 1970's to include three levels, expanded into literature for small ensembles and began a new focus in the elementary classroom via recorder. Watching him teach at conventions, clinics and in summer band classes was a joy. He had so much information about teaching young band students and he worked well with young band directors.

In 1996 I began teaming with Ed Sueta in his summer outreach programs at both the College of St. Catherine and at Villanova University. In addition, I traveled to a number of conventions to work with both he, his son, Eddie, and his daughter, Julie. Together they provide a beautiful team and I was so impressed with the contributions they were making in the lives of thousands of music teachers and millions of music students on an annual basis with heir printed materials and recorders.

As I continue to work with Ed Sueta, I consider our teaming together a dramatic coincidence and a major part of my journey. When I see Ed Sueta and his outreach to help teachers help students, I see myself. As such, I feel his strong commitment, dedication and devotion to music as a discipline that reaches out and saves the emotional lives of so many people. Ed Sueta is a spiritual man. He is a professional's professional. God connected me with Ed Sueta, and this connection helped me to realize my calling, my journey and my destiny in life.

~ KATHRYN DEARBORN ~

In 1994 CAMERATA FINE ARTS, INC. was created and flourished throughout most of the 1990's as the premier orchestral program for young musicians in La Porte and Porter counties in the state of Indiana. This was a superhuman effort by all involved, as a wonderful team of the most angelic people beginning with the students and their families came together thirsty for a taste of an outstanding classical arts experience. Kathryn Dearborn was the soul of this outreach and an angel who is best understood by her beautiful Credo which reads as follows:

We consider our earnest purpose a dedicated mission: to enrich the lives of children and youth through the greatness and beauty of the fine arts.

We believe knowledge and appreciation of classical music, literature, drama, dance, and art which have endured through the ages serve to uplift the spirit, instill the right values, and unify generations.

We also believe that those given the responsibility of imparting the joy and discipline required for excellence in the arts have the solemn duty to live their lives in a way which provides wholesome and exemplary leadership for children and youth.

This leadership means living above petty, self-aggrandizing words and actions, abiding by the Golden Rule, and respecting each other and each student for his unique individual worth.

In order to ensure the ideals of the Camerata Fine Arts Program, those who join the endeavor should be in agreement with the philosophy of Camerata and abide by its artistic and ethical standards.

Kathryn also wrote a beautiful statement of education philosophy and a procedure for everyone to voice their grievances if and when there were concerns. We all learned and were highly inspired by her writing and the passion that she exemplified on a daily basis. Her heart and her soul reached out to the Camerata family and will always be in the hearts and minds of all who touched her life. There are angels and there are angels. I thank God for the privilege of meeting Kathryn Dearborn and for the opportunity to know and feel her inspiration and spirituality.

~ SUMMARY ~

The sequence of my mentors span from 1957 through the present. Each mentor came into my life at the exact time I needed each one of them. I continue their legacies with my energy and outreach. It is my destiny to continue to perform my daily duets with God and learn from the children and the music; and to give as much as possible to those who want to listen.

It has taken 52 years to realize the priorities, to understand how to hear God and to know that God is in all of us. Knowing how important the children of God are and knowing how beautifully music moves the soul, I have been blessed to be able to focus on both music and children as the core of my life. I am grateful to be able to understand how the children, the music and my mentors continue to shape my life, give me spiritual strength and give me vision to help others.

By sharing this story of my mentors and their wisdom that guided me through each step of my spiritual journey, I hope to inspire others to write their story and to share their journey. With this sharing the next generation can understand the synergy of spirituality that will continue to bond and connect us all regardless of our differences. It is the bonding, the connection and the synergy across all cultural and religious barriers that must continue to be our primary mission for future generations.

CHAPTER THREE

The Vision: Help the Teachers Help the Children

During my first seven years of public school music teaching in Connecticut I learned that the number one problem in the classroom was the absences of a program to nurture teachers. It occurred to me one day that the idea of graduating from an accredited college or university with a teaching degree at age 22 and retiring at age 65 created a void of 43 years with only on requirement between: obtain 30 hours of graduate credits towards a masters degree over a ten-year period of time.

In the early seventies there was a paradox in the circle of teaching and learning. Those who became tired of teaching moved on to a college or university in their geographic area to teach part time or full time in education. At a time in their life when they were most discouraged about their work in the classroom, they moved on to influence a group of young motivated music students who quickly became uninspired with their method classes at the university level. As such, these young inspired students who were being uninspired found themselves searching for mentors in the field who could motivate them.

Looking at course curriculums at music schools in the early seventies, I found little interest and little concern about pragmatic problems of music teachers in the classroom in grades K-12. There were few university faculty connected to the dynamics of classroom music teaching in grades K-12.

The challenge was three-fold:

a) To wake-up the schools of higher education who were charged with the responsibility of training music teachers and demonstrate to them what they should do to help the music teaching profession on an annual basis.

b) Alert the experts who were disconnected from those local music teachers across the country.

c) To encourage local music teachers (who were desperate for the ideas, strategies, materials and literature that they did not receive in their teacher-training days) to register for summer music courses with pragmatic topics and outstanding clinicians.

It took me from 1969 to 1977 to be in a position to begin to work on the three-fold challenge. At this point I had worked in the public schools of East and West Hartford, Connecticut and Pittsfield, Massachusetts while working part-time at the Hartt School of Music and Trinity College. These multiple opportunities gave me the bigger picture of the problem as I worked with outstanding individuals who were nationally recognized for their expertise in specific aspects of music education, including: conducting, elementary methods, band, orchestra, choir, literature, rehearsal techniques, instrument repair and music theater.

In 1977 I was 30 years old, a K-12 director of music and working with an outstanding team of school administrators. Fortunately, this team of administrators under the direction of Henry Schoebel were creative, innovative and created the time each Wednesday of the school year to nurture their staff by closing school at 1:30 p.m.! Suddenly, I found myself in the perfect position to meet all three challenges.

a) I could establish a national model called THE FALL WORKSHOPS FOR MUSIC EDUCATORS funded by the Glastonbury Public Schools' In-Service Account.

b) It would include all the music teachers in Glastonbury plus invited guests from throughout Connecticut.

c) Area universities and colleges could see that the outstanding teachers in the area were providing the instruction as these leaders had the information.

In the fall of 1977, 1978, 1979 and 1980 we continued the series of the fall workshops with leading music educators in the field providing the instruction. Quickly, we found that the formula for success was as follows:

a) The guest clinician needed to be someone who was working in the specific area of expertise on a daily basis in a school setting.

b) The guest clinicians needed to provide the teachers with materials that they could implement in their respective classrooms immediately: songs, games, literature, ideas and problem-solving ideas as needs were expressed by the teachers.

c) There needed to be time at each workshop where the music teachers could vent their concerns, frustrations, successes, failures and disappointments of the week.

d) We need to have 6 consecutive Wednesdays of workshops with the finale a SHARING WORKSHOP where each teacher shared their best lesson plan.

In January of 1981 Donald Harris, Dean of Hartt School of Music invited me to create a summer workshop series for graduate credit for their 1981 SUMMERTERM Program based on the success of the Fall Workshop Series in the Glastonbury Public Schools. Evaluations written by the teachers to the clinicians revealed a deep appreciation for the opportunity to have this summer series. By the end of the summer we knew that we were meeting a need and had created a new dimension: Help the teachers help the children with new ideas, materials, literature and new techniques for graduate credit .

The format was a win-win for all involved. The Hartt School of Music was receiving national attention for a new, creative and innovative music program for teachers, the SUMMER TERM PROGRAM and it was able to show a profit, the teachers were able to obtain graduate credit for very pragmatic courses that would help them in their annual preparation for their students, and most importantly, everyone felt good that we as a team were doing the right things at the right time for the teachers.

In hindsight, I am not sure how I knew, why I knew, or where I knew what to do. I just knew and did! The opportunities to develop this concept just came to me in sequence as if this was the script.

First, my role in the script was to make everything happen, bring everyone together and enjoy the results of the effort. Secondly, my role was not to become financially wealthy, or to incorporate the program, or to strive for fame with the concept. Finally, my role was to contribute my talents and vision and learn from the experience.

This modest beginning of the three-fold plan to help teachers help students has expanded to include a large network of universities who believe strongly in this philosophy of helping teachers help students in music education. The modeling that began at the Hartt School of music has been very contagious. Most would reflect that this was a very missionary effort in the field of music education.

There always will be a need for this concept in music education and I would encourage others in the fields of languages, sciences, math, history, art and physical education to provide similar opportunities for teachers in the K-12 public school curriculum. Teachers are the soul of civilization beginning with parents, school teachers, religious teachers, coaches, scout leaders and civic youth leaders.

It is important that all these individuals have the highest respect of our communities as they have the most important responsibilities in educating and modeling for our children. It is important that we strongly encourage individual teachers to take courses to upgrade their skills.

Also, it is important that the content of the courses offered are relevant to the needs of the teachers and their students. Finally, the choice of clinicians or professors teaching the courses need to be individuals who are at present having successful experiences with children, schools and school programs.

CHAPTER FOUR

The Angels Nurture the Teacher from Day to Day

Teachers live a very isolated professional life. There is little time in the normal course of a school day for teachers to interact with colleagues or administrators. The main focus of the teacher's life is their students. this relationship is special, spiritual and meaningful.

The age of the children, the course being taught, the length of time the teacher spends with children and the size of the class determines the type of relationship that is established between a teacher and each child in a class. Although the same age, children are so different in many ways. However, for the teacher, he learning style of a child is most important as is the level of academic support and emotional support the child is receiving at home from their parents.

As I find myself teaching middle school music in a public school setting on a daily basis, I have a variety of class topics, class sizes and academic abilities in music education. The students I work with daily are different in age, culture and artistic background with some students coming to class with a strong background in music skills and others with very little skills or knowledge about music. Regardless of individual student's level of attitude, ability and self-esteem, I have enjoyed reaching these students spiritually by giving everyone an opportunity to develop their musical talents to their maximum potential. many students are surprised at the middle school level that they have real musical talent and can demonstrate that talent on a daily basis in class.

Students who are in bands or orchestras are expected to rent or buy their own instrument to bring; however, talented students who cannot afford an instrument are left out. many educators in the 20th century felt that instrumental music was elitist and they are probably correct from one prospective. However, the tradition of beginning a musical instrument is considered to be one of the cultural birthrights in many families and in many cultures; thus, the tradition continues with the parents supporting the bulk of the burden of cost, enforcing practice time at home, purchasing books and funding private institutions.

In communities where budgets are low but the talent is high , schools can help students with programs in guitar, percussion and computerized music via music technology. This approach for some students combined with the traditional band, orchestra and choir program gives students at the middle school level an equal opportunity to discover their talent. The combination to unlock their "treasure chest of talent" is simply believe they have talent and go with the flow of energy as the music class progresses from day to day with the development of basic skills. As students experience success in class, it is amazing to observe the kinds of positive initiatives they will take in class. Daily extra credit via solo performances, small group performance, helping or teaming with other struggling students or learning a new tune are all very motivating for students and keeps their skills moving to the next level. verbally, students will initiate interesting questions or share a family experience with their instruments. Other students give concerts at home and parents write a review of their performance.

At the middle school level, much of the student communication is non-verbal. It is exciting to see how comfortable middle school students are with non-verbal communication, and how clearly students of all abilities can communicate in-depth to the teacher and classmates by their attitude, facial expression, personal performance, body language and eye contact. Students who are using school music equipment are at first overwhelmed that they have an instrument of their own to use in school for the length of the music program.

The skill level in music performance at the middle school level is wide-ranging but the appreciation by the students for the opportunity to learn a musical instrument is also wide-ranging. Students who view themselves as non-talented musicians, low academic achievers, inferior to other students in class need the teacher's encouragement the most. It is often this group of students who provide the teacher with the most powerful spiritual impact from day to day. In addition, this group includes the largest quantity of angels who deeply appreciate the teacher's efforts.

Too often academic teachers give their lower achieving students the wrong message via body language, voice tone, attitude and favoritism. As this reality occurs, the music teacher has the opportunity via music performance to help a student's self-esteem. It is important for students to know that you value them as people regardless of the speed at which they learn a skill.

Most teachers wait two seconds for their answers. Lower achieving students may have the answer but cannot demonstrate that achievement in two seconds. Teachers need to wait seven to ten seconds for their answers. It is amazing what those few additional seconds reveal. Most teachers miss the spiritual opportunity and so the lower achieving students.

In too many school settings COMPETITION is the center of the learning experience regardless of the course topic in curricular and extra-curricular opportunities. Music is not about competition but about learning to work together, listening together and creating musical sounds that are in harmony with each other. Music is like a magnet attracting students to work together to enjoy the art form.

Enjoying music is like enjoying food, nature, the universe, sleep and friends. The beauty of music is like the beauty of nature. One can learn and enjoy music for a lifetime. Music is not like doing required homework in preparation for quizzes or tests. Music skills can be used throughout life and bring great joy and happiness to individuals who are actively involved in music performance.

Music is not an academic course. It is an aesthetic course. Music requires students to strive for perfection and in addition, the result has to have the appropriate emotion and style. In this setting students have the opportunity to exercise their emotional and psychological intelligence, their leadership skills and expand their skills in their areas of problem-solving and conflict management between students. Many life skills will include non-verbal skills, spiritual skills, emotional skills and psychological skills. Music courses emphasize all of these skills in addition to the academic skills.

As a music teacher, I gradually increased my awareness of the many non-verbal and non-academic communications in my ten different classes each week. I shifted my role from the director of the class to the connector of the class: connecting students, ideas, emotions, successes and improving effort on a daily basis. Students were understanding the skill expectation in my classes and the deadlines for testing, but in the process of preparation there was a "victory garden" of thoughts, emotion, excitement, experiments, new successes and increased risk-taking.

At the middle school level the biggest fear is embarrassment; thus, any new concept, idea or musical instrument performance is "red-alert" for most students. After a few weeks students in all my classes became relaxed about testing, extra-credit and new skill levels. The fears of failure and embarrassment diminish quickly and students begin understanding and believing that they, in fact, do have a treasure chest of talent that needs to be opened. Students understand that they have always had this talent but were disconnected from their musical talent. Seeing and feeling this transformation in every classroom with students between the ages of 11 and 14 is magical and spiritual at the same time.

The ultimate spiritual experience in class is watching students successfully teach and motivate other students. When I am working with students at the middle school level, I emphasize that the most important thing they do with their musical talent is teach at least one other person their knowledge of and skills in music. Students in our school are the best teachers of the elementary school students about our music program at the middle school level. Elementary school students are motivated by what they hear their older brothers or sisters students or by cousins in the community. Students believe what this network of students say regardless of what adults say.

Observing students helping other students with their music performance skills is a total joy! I continue to stress that the teacher is the person with the information who wants to share it, and the student is the person without the information who wants to learn the information. In my classroom the topic is music; however, in another classroom with another academic subject one of my music students could teach me what they have just learned. The best teachers are the best students and the teacher's knowledge and respect for this circle of learning and teaching is paramount for the highest level of understanding.

Students are sensitive to the teacher's level of respect, understanding and caring of students. The teacher's skill in a course is important, but the teacher's ability to show empathy, compassion and patience towards all students is the main thing. It is important for teachers to keep the main thing, the main thing. I try to have good eye contact and positive body language which helps my students stay in sync with what I am doing. Every student is vitally important and every student's effort, improvement, attitude and increased ability in every class is evaluated by the teacher and the students.

At first, many students want to tell you what they cannot do. I am interested only with what they can do and build on that level of skill development. Being positive, believing in the students' skills in music and demonstrating sincere caring about each student's skill development is what the teaching and learning process is all about. Students need to know why music is important in their life and they need to understand that everyone has a talent in music.

Music allows the teacher to accept the student exactly where have developed to date in their life. The music teacher's acceptance of each student gives each student the opportunity to show appreciation to their music teacher. This is the flow of spiritual energy when I know my teaching is at the highest level.

In the high school and college years most students will compete, be tracked by ability, compete for jobs and compete for scholarships at colleges and universities. The higher calling for teachers and students is the spiritual connection and the belief the teacher has in the student. With this high level of emotional intelligence the teacher draws out of the students an angelic flow of universal understanding. This allows both the teacher and student to share the euphoric experience of happiness and love for each

other and for the art of music that bonds them together
eternally.

CHAPTER FIVE

Angelic Sounds: Spiritual Gifts from the Students to the Teacher

As I began my thirtieth year of teaching music, I made a commitment each day to hear and receive at least one spiritual gift from one or more of my students. Each day there were students who were in one of the following categories:

a) PURE ANGELS: Students who radiate spiritual energy when they arrive to class.

b) SPIRITUAL ANGELS: Students who share their spiritual energy with other students.

c) POTENTIAL ANGELS: Students who with more time and more self-confidence will share their spiritual gifts in class.

The "pure angels" are students who are talented musically, want to share their talent but are not driven by ego, selfishness or competition. Pure angels want to be appreciated, discovered and nurtured by the music teacher and class. Pure angels perform beautifully in class at all times and are role models by their example. Our angels are seldom flustered, upset or discouraged and they have a very, very strong spiritual center.

The "spiritual angels" are good students who love music, practice daily, expect high achievement from themselves, enjoy school and are eager to demonstrate their skills. These students are calm, steady, consistent and have a strong self-image. I can always call on these students to help and share with other students, try something new or take a musical risk in front of the class without embarrassment.

The "potential angels" are students who are missing any one or more of the following skills in their school music performance: reading skills, attitude, self-discipline, working well with other students, working well with the music teacher, working at home with their daily practice or positive work ethic. Over the years I have learned to be very patient with this group and to understand that this group is where the teacher needs to spend more time with the students and develop more patience.

It is great to have champions, leaders and models in class, but the reality is that most of these students come to you in class with these learned at home and most likely could progress without your input. However, students who are disconnected may drop-out of music during the school year, become discouraged or feel you do not understand their inner feelings about music. Simply, these students need more time and I, as the music teacher, need to be much, much more patient. Their gifts and spiritual energy will flow but not until the end of the school year or until the next.

When students in this third category share their spiritual energy with you, they share their feelings with you from their soul with a joy that is unmatched in the first two categories. The euphoria of the student's success helps develop more patience. Being patient with the disconnected student is a difficult skill for most teachers, especially if they are product-oriented.

During this past year, I had a student who was next to last chair in one of my bands. he was a good student but just could not put together all the skills necessary for a good test performance. His mother called me one day to say that she was having her son work with her brother and hoped I would hear a difference during the last few weeks of school.

In our final round of testing, the student played his test almost perfectly. The band students spontaneously applauded and the student had the widest smile of the year on his face. This was the sweetest "angelic sound" of the year for me, and the "angelic sound" I waited the longest to hear.

Three talented 7th grade band members had demonstrated exceptional talent throughout the year. they each were pure angels. In the school band program they repeatedly performed outstanding test scores, performed as soloists throughout the year and were wonderful role models for the others in the band. As the final weeks of the school year approached, they asked if I had any trio music for them to play together. I was pleased that I did have music for them and if they would like to play as a trio, I would be glad to feature them next year at our 8th Grade Winter Band Concert.

The next morning at 7:45 a.m. all three students appeared in the band room ready to work out the details of their new trio. Having these three students find each other and want to enrich their musicianship by performing together was the most sophisticated "angelic" experience of the year for me.

With any beginning band program, the band director is stressing the importance of practicing every day. In my classes, I compare their new instrument to spending time with their best friend. The one thing in common about friends is that they spend a lot of time together and are excited about being together. This experience with friendship begins with families and branches out into the community.

One day a trio of 6th graders approached me with an exaggeration of the above metaphor: they wanted to have their respective instrument marry each other and adopt one child! After much discussion the students wrote up the marriage ceremony and the adoption papers and to my surprise the instruments to be married, an oboe (who was the groom) and the flute

(who was the bride,) arrived to class fully clothed in appropriate attire. With this came the adopted child, a piccolo!

There was a ceremony, a witness (the 6th grade band class) and a reception with lollipops! In thirty years of teaching, this was the first time students raised the level of animation to this height. I do not expect to see this level of creativity, bonding and animation again in any of my classes.

One Saturday afternoon I was practicing at home and the phone rang. On the line was one of my 6th grade saxophonists who was calling me at home long distance. He went to a military band concert last evening and he was chosen out of the audience to guest conduct the band on the final selection of the evening. He was calling to tell me that he was very surprised to be selected and felt that being "on the spot" he would do his best to imitate my style of conducting.

He proceeded to explain how he began, his gestures, his beat pattern and his eye contact with the musicians. Finally, he said, "Mr. Allen, I tried to conduct just like you."

A new student arrived to our middle school with a terrific talent. As months progressed she was able to develop her piano skills with our advanced jazz band program while at the same time develop her mallet skills on the xylophone. Every grading period each band student tests on a preselected piece of music in front of the entire band. Having done this routine for many years, one experiences many surprises in each section of the band.

However, when this one xylophone student performed, the entire band came to a spiritual silence before, during and after her performance. The silence was like none I have ever heard before in any class. Simple, the band knew this student had a gift from God and the students were giving her and God the respect they jointly deserved. This event occurred repeatedly during the school year.

Annually, I test approximately 160 students twelve times during the school year. Never have I experienced such a mystical experience as this single student's performance. What has been amazing to me is the non-verbal recognition of this student's spiritual gift of music. All students understand it while no one has ever verbalized their reaction to this repeated experience in class.

In my exploratory music classes I had a very talented student who did extremely well in both guitar and percussion classes. At the end of the year we have a two-day MUSIC EXTRAVANGANZA featuring guest artists. This student asked if he could perform the one tune he had been working on at home. He went beyond the guitar class, purchased an electric guitar and was encouraged at home to perform.

Although he was very nervous, this talented student performed as part of the MUSIC EXTRAVANGANZA. Since this beginning event, he has performed annually with a style of his own and many of his own compositions. He is an excellent role model and hopes to enroll in a major music school after high school. This student never spent a day in band, orchestra or choir as he prefers solo performing over participating in a large ensemble.

Recently, a most talented student set the school record for the most superior performances at contest: trumpet, brass trio, voice, vocal trio and piano. In addition, this student was the lead trumpet with the jazz band, performed a concerto-style solo with band accompaniment and sang at the annual MUSIC EXTRAVAGANZA.

This was the first time in thirty years that I experienced such a gifted music student at the middle school extend her talents and gifts to the maximum level of expectation. In addition I had never experienced such an effort by a school in responding to her talent with repeated opportunities for her to perform.

I had the privilege of working with Bruce Foote in the 1980's. He developed a terrific program for young band performers in Marlboro, Connecticut. I invited him to do an afternoon workshop for a team of band directors in Connecticut and he was pleased to be our clinician for the afternoon. I was totally unprepared for the impact Bruce made on each of us at this single workshop. At the very beginning of the workshop he opened with the following:

"I always wanted to be a music educator s a youngster. I feel God has touched my life by giving me the opportunity to serve children through music. I am so proud to be a music teacher."

I had never heard a music teacher before nor have I heard a music teacher since make such a powerful public statement about the quality of their personal life and the quality of their professional life. I always felt that Bruce was a very spiritual person and approached his professional commitments with that same depth.

During the 1976-77 school year I met a wonderful clarinetist who was a senior at Taconic High School. She had not performed in a school band since middle school as Taconic High School had a 6-period day during her first three years there. However, she loved music and was interested in becoming involved in our start-up band at Taconic High School.

As I was able to spend more time with this talented student, I was aware that she was interested in music as a career and needed help with some connections to the University of Massachusetts. Within weeks we had the clarinet teacher visit the band and this student was able to hear the inside scoop on the music education program at the University of Massachusetts and what the entrance requirements would include.

Over the next three months I worked hard to prepare her for the entrance tests: academic, music theory and clarinet performance skills. To her surprise she was accepted! I was thrilled but knew that her family situation was such that she would need a large financial package.

To a large degree, this student was on her own in her pursuits of a music education degree at the University of Massachusetts. We both were excited to hear she would receive enough financial aid to begin in the fall of 1977. As time progressed, she completed both a Bachelor of Music Education Degree and a Masters Degree in Conducting.

The relationship we developed as a student and teacher during the 1976-77 school year was one of the most profound experiences in my thirty years of teaching. As I was only at Taconic High School on year and commuted daily 180 miles round trip, I felt God had sent me to Pittsfield to help this one student as well as start up their new band program.

This student's commitment to music education, her academic accomplishments at the University of Massachusetts and her success in this transition from high school to the university level was a wonderful experience. I was grateful to be in a position to help this student. Her commitment and dedication changed my life forever.

As these "angelic sounds" from the students appeared in my life as a music teacher, I was immediately aware that God had His hand on the rudder guiding each experience and was talking to me through the students and their respective experiences. These experiences did not involve any competitions for the first place or involve parents pushing their children to excel. The students connected to their talent, totally enjoyed their skill progress and developed their talents in a logical and natural flow.

It is these angelic experiences of joy that I continue to receive from students that keeps the learning process at a very high level of understanding and retention. Other angelic experiences are as simple as a smile or a positive comment by a struggling student or special eye contact. The student is sending their love with each success they are having in the learning process and it is important for the student to know that the teacher is listening and receiving their expression of thanks with appreciation and love.

In my earlier years of teaching I was too busy achieving the goal of the class or performing group to recognize the "angelic sounds" and the "angelic outreach" of each student to my teaching. That was a mistake. Such sounds come from all directions, from all types of students, with no preparation and with lots of love.

Being prepared to hear these sounds and know that they are going to appear in every class in a random pattern has changed my life as a teacher. God continues to work through children, and God continues to work through music every minute of every day.

Being aware that I, as a teacher, am being encouraged by the students to connect to their spiritual energy has changed my life.

CHAPTER SIX

The Gifted and Talented Angels

In preparing for the fifth decade of teaching, I continue to be most concerned about the lives of the gifted and talented children. Society is so careful to lock-step children by age as they move through life even though the talent of a gifted and talented child may not match their chronological age. I have had the opportunity to work with many gifted and talented students from week to week spanning the ages of 7-22. In almost every case I felt that each individual student was not receiving the support network necessary to nurture their advanced level needs.

Within the "gifted and talented" label there are many subdivisions including: academically talented, artistically talented, musically talented, athletically talented and technologically talented. In addition there are students who have a wonderful "sixth sense" about things and about life. These students are very calm and quiet about their unique gift, but it is clear that they have a wonderful insight into the lives of individuals and the future.

In public school settings there is a small percentage of gifted and talented students. Wherever possible specific public schools attempt to address the needs of these students at the middle school and high school levels with advance placement classes in specific core subjects; however, schools are not structured to individualize any aspect of the comprehensive curriculum to any specific segment of the student population.

In some communities there are civic organizations, churches and talented individuals who can work with students one-to-one as a coach, trainer or tutor outside the school day. In such cases it is the parents who recognize the talent and want their child to have the very best instruction as soon as possible. It is the parents' insight and the commitment of these highly trained individuals that combine to make the difference in the lives of gifted and talented children.

Too often gifted and talented students are pulled too hard in too many directions on a daily basis with no one present to manage the "big picture." As a result, there are too many children who become very ill with the stress and strain of the expectations from all their teachers and coaches. With a disappointment that includes a large number of days absent from school, too many gifted and talented students have to back off and slow down their many high-level activities.

It is important for gifted and talented students to stay focused, stay balanced and to understand their talent and their priorities on a daily basis. Many students need help with this throughout their school life. Parents and mentors are critical to help keep each child balanced.

The following experiences with gifted and talented students permanently changed my vision, my priorities and my attitude about the importance of helping students with their lives through music teaching.

~JULIANNE ~

Julianne was a beginning clarinet student in my beginning band class at Hopewell Elementary School in Glastonbury, Connecticut. She was very bright, extremely talented and wanting to play the clarinet. She excelled over all the other students in band and by the spring concert I was featuring her as much as possible. As she began her second year, we moved her to a more challenging instrument: the French horn. As her second year progressed, she confided in me that she wanted to play the violin, but her mother did not like the violin and did not want the violin sound in the house!

Continuing with the French horn through 9th grade Julianne auditioned for the solo competition with the Hartford Symphony Orchestra and to no one's surprise she won the competition excelling beyond many older high school students. With this successful solo performance she still yearned to play a string instrument and soon began taking private lessons on the contrabass at the Hartt School of Music.

Within a three year period she auditioned to attend the Hartt School of Music and received a full scholarship to study with the world-renowned bassist, Gary Karr. This experience came full circle and I better understood the power of parents in their attitudes toward music and musical instruments. At the same time, I discovered that the determination and persistence of talented young musicians to achieve in music at their highest level of talent is of the highest importance and priority.

~ BOB ~

Bob was a talented 9th grade oboist who traveled over 50 miles round trip each week to take private lesson with me on Monday evenings at 7:00 p.m. I found Bob extremely bright and very bonded to music and the oboe. Within a few months it was clear that Bob was going to include music as a major part of his life after high school. Towards the end of his junior year Bob was concerned as his father and uncles were all engineers and Bob was considering a double major in college: pre-med and oboe! This had the family upset to the point that they requested a family meeting with me and Bob during Bob's lesson time.

As a result, the entire family came with all the uncles to Bob's lesson one chilly October evening. The family needed help understanding what an oboist did in life, what type of money they earned and the possibilities for a job after college. After considerable discussion the family left, and I felt that with the information presented they were hoping Bob would change his mind!

As the months progressed, Bob enrolled at Case Wester Reserve University where he was a double major in both pre-med and oboe. He achieved a 4.0 average on both majors and proceeded back to Connecticut where he began his formal medical training at the University of Connecticut and married Lauren, the oboe student that followed his lesson on Monday evenings at 7:30 p.m.!

~ TRACEY ~

Tracey was a spiritual student with many gifts including oboe performance. I can remember the day her father purchased her Loree oboe, top of the line and most expensive. Beginning her instrumental career as a flutist, Tracey quickly moved to the oboe where she excelled through high school. She, her good friend Nancy, and myself played trios in the area and eventually recorded a cassette tape titled "OBOE ALIVE" and a second cassette titled "OBOE AND STRINGS ALIVE." In addition, we performed on the Rovert Lurtsemer Show in Boston where we went into the studio with composer Robert Edward Smith and performed a trio on WGBH radio in Boston and performed a new piece of music dedicated to Tracey's mom who had recently passed on.

I can remember that February afternoon when Tracey arrived at her oboe lesson overwhelmed with grief. her mother had been positively diagnosed with lung cancer. I could tell that the news was very bad and that her mother had a limited time to live. As the months progressed her mother declined. She was one of the most vital and energetic women I had ever met. Thus, it was almost impossible to believe that she was facing a fatal situation in her young life. Our trio continued to perform in the area and Tracey's mom drove herself to each performance through the month of May. In June she passed on.

Not knowing she passed on the night before, I called to the house and Tracey's father answered the phone. I asked him how things were going and the silence of the next few seconds was so spiritually powerful. No words were necessary.

The entire community was crushed and overwhelmed with grief. A traditional funeral took place with a viewing, religious service and burial. It was a family tradition for members of the family to make a presentation at the funeral. Our trio performed seated next to the casket. Tracey performed the 1st oboe part to the second movement of Opus 87a by Beethoven for two oboes and English horn. She did not miss a note!

As all the activities surrounding the funeral took place, Tracey at age 16 was the rock! She remained strong and gave to others strength. I told her at many lessons that she would be the first woman President of the United States. I felt that it was appropriate to have a piece of music written in honor of her mother. Robert Edward Smith wrote "DIVERTIMENTO" for two oboes and an English horn. One year later there was a tribute to Tracey's mom featuring our premiere piece.

Following the performance, Tracey's father stood up in the audience to thank the composer and the trio for such an outstanding performance and proceeded to emotionally break down. I walked back to him and hugged him as an expression of my love and caring for him and his family. At that moment, Tracey broke down and cried. During this entire experience, I was very concerned about Tracey and she expressed to me that the days were fine; however, the nights were very difficult. Tracey continued to fight for crusades to raise money for cancer in her mother's name and took one coast to coast bike trip as her contribution towards the fight to cure cancer.

I have kept Tracey's picture on my wall and have said a prayer daily for her and her family since the day her mother passed on. With this experience I felt the spiritual power of music and how it bonds a teacher with a student beyond words or any human experience. I thank God that I met Tracey and her family. Our relationship as teacher and student was a dramatic, life-changing experience for me that was no accidental coincidence.

~ MEGAN ~

Unlike the normal one semester or one year teaching pattern that a teacher develops with his or her students from pre-school through graduate school, the private music teacher has the opportunity to have an ongoing relationship with a private music student from the beginning days with an instrument (usually 5th or 6th grade) through their senior year of high school. This relationship becomes very special, very personal and very important to both the student and the teacher. The bonding is deep and the commitment is very strong.

Megan was a very unique talent who began oboe lessons in the 6th grade with an impressive background on the piano prior to beginning the oboe. From the beginning I knew that Megan, with strong support from her immediate and extended family, was going to be a wonderful model for other younger oboists as her oboe career progressed.

Throughout her middle school years, Megan progressed rapidly with her musical and oboe skills. She attended summer camps, performed in bands and orchestras, received regional and statewide honors for her performances on both oboe and English horn and performed with the Chicago Youth Symphony Orchestra including a European tour. In her senior year she gave a full-length recital that would have qualified for a Senior Recital at the undergraduate level of a music observatory. The literature she selected, those accompanying her, and the level of the performance combined to make her recital as a high school senior a major musical event that attracted many oboists in the area.

Megan was accepted as an oboe performance major at the University of Iowa which accepts only two oboe majors per year and she continues to study in the summer in Europe. This type of progress from 6th grade through the undergraduate level is the modeling all students in music need, especially the oboists! O always thought of Megan as a spiritually motivated student and her love of music combined with her natural ability was such a wonderful gift that inspired all who knew her and worked with her in music performance.

~ STEPHANIE ~

Stephanie took private oboe lessons with me from 6th through 12th grade. She was a most talented academic student ranking #5 in her class of over 500 students and a most talented oboist who worked very hard to achieve her artistic accomplishments throughout the high school years in the areas of solo performance, chamber music, band and orchestra. Wanting to be an architect, Stephanie received scholarship to Notre Dame University where she performs in the University Symphony Orchestra.

During her senior year of high school, Stephanie joined the top 10% of her class in selecting the two teachers who most influenced her during her 12 years in school. I was one of her choices! What an honor it was to be selected. There are times in a teacher's life when a student or student's initiate thoughts, ideas or gratitude changes a teacher's life forever.

Although I thanked Stephanie repeatedly, it was difficult for me to adequately express how much Stephanie's selection affected me personally and professionally. Teaching is a two-way street. The teacher can give to the student or students, but there needs to be equal giving back to the teacher by the student or students. Many times teachers do not receive that love in return and at other times the students extend themselves far beyond what the teacher expects. These are the "angelic experiences" of teaching not found in most professions.

~ VALERIE ~

There are few "trail blazing" students who go beyond what one would expect; however, when it does happen, it is important to reflect with the student on how important their efforts are in setting the pace for future students who will follow their footsteps.

I met Valerie in the summer before her senior year of high school. It was immediately clear that she was a most gifted musician who loved music and had a special talent for both the oboe and English horn. She studied oboe with me during her senior year and decided to enroll at the university where I taught oboe.

Valerie enrolled as an oboe performance major! The significance of this decision was impressive as she would be the first oboe performance major to graduate from this university in its long history of excellence in music. The university traditionally graduated performance majors in organ, piano and voice; however, an oboe performance major was a new dimension to the total vision of the music department.

As Valerie progressed through her performance degree in oboe, she experienced a variety of challenges, a junior recital and a senior recital. All of these experiences were new to her and none of these challenges were easy for her. However, she worked through the challenges, the upsets and the disappointments to accomplish her goal: to graduate as the first-ever oboe performance major at the university.

~ HELEN ~

As previously mentioned, a special aspect of private music teaching is for a teacher to work with his or her students from their first lesson in 6th grade to their final lesson in grade 12; however, Helen extended this experience for the first time in my 30-year experience as a private oboe teacher. Helen studied with me from grades 6 to 13.

She demonstrated a beautiful talent in both oboe and English horn performance. At the same time, she has a lovely voice and is a wonderful actress. After seven years of studying with me on both the oboe and English horn, Helen enrolled in the local university where I teach oboe and will continue studying with me as her private instructor for an 8th consecutive year.

~JULIA ~

Spirituality is an important aspect in the life of all the top performers in both the performing arts and in athletic competition. Julia was a student who studied with me during her junior and senior year of high school. her lessons were very spiritual for me.

Regardless of her mood, her preparation or the literature being performed, Julia approached her performance from a deep spiritual level. She was always calm, introspective, at peace and performed with a heavenly sound. She had a wonderful vibrato on both the oboe and English horn and her phrasing was most beautiful.

I often shared my feeling about her performance on both double reed instruments. her approach to performance was most exciting, interesting and compelling. After high school she purchased a beautiful oboe and pursued her performance at the university level as she majored in education. There are too few students who approach their performance from their soul. Julia was able to do this with a natural flow and her aura at every lesson was most angelic. Seeing the angel in your students is sometimes difficult; however, with Julia, she was the ultimate angel.

I was so happy to be able to share my enthusiasm for Julia's talent at her weekly lesson. The art of music performance gave Julia an opportunity to release her angelic talent at the highest level.

~ SONYA ~

Sonya was a talented oboist. She studied with me in her high school years while being a most talented gymnast. During her lessons I became aware that Sonya was struggling in her personal life. One evening I received a call from her parents saying that Sonya needed help and was struggling emotionally with a variety of problems. The parents indicated that Sonya was in an emergency situation emotionally and felt I was the one adult in her life who could help her.

Feeling inadequate but most concerned for Sonya, I proceeded to send my first letter to her outlining all the positive things in her life and how much I appreciated her talent and vision on life's many ups and downs. For two weeks I sent Sonya a number of positive letters. Finally, she showed up to her oboe lesson and I never felt more relieved. We both know that something special happened between the two of us during this crisis and all of the lessons that followed were filled with joy, enthusiasm and caring of the highest order.

This was a most spiritual experience for me and I knew that we both were on a more spiritual level as teacher and student. Sonya did well with her oboe performance through high school, but I have not been in contact with her for a number of years. I know when

I see her, we will share that same depth of spirituality we shared five years ago.

CHAPTER SEVEN

The Struggling Angels

In most secondary school music programs (grades 6-12) students are being tracked by their level of interest in music, talent in music, and parental financial support for their child in music. The top level finds the students playing band and string instruments. The second level finds students singing in the choir program. The third level finds students in an exploratory music program of non-performers which in our school is a 100% hands-on program where students are making music and developing musical skills via recorder, guitar and percussion instruments.

If a student is interested in learning how to play a band or string orchestra instrument via the middle school music program, the student must first have the support of his parents who will buy or rent an instrument, purchase a book, provide private lessons and support the child at home each day in the daily practice routine. However, many students with musical talent find themselves struggling alone with no interest at home in their musical talent and growth and no interest in providing the appropriate instrument where the child can have success. These students are THE STRUGGLING ANGELS!"

When I first meet with my percussion and guitar classes, the students are grouped in classes of 20-26 students. One group of classes are in the 7th grade and another group of classes are in the 8th grade. Beginning with the 7th graders in percussion class, I begin by telling all the students that EACH ONE OF YOU HAS MUSICAL TALENT!

Finding your musical talent requires three things:

a)	A musical instrument being provided by the school.

b)   A music teacher to help you each week with your skills and talent.

c)   A set schedule each week to develop your skills and talents.

Each student learns that the key to learning a musical instrument is to treat it like your best friend or your best stuff animal or your best living pet at home! With strong affection towards the instrument of choice, a student makes rapid progress with all the needs falling into place naturally: practicing daily, learning from the students and teacher at school, and performing concerts at school, home and church.

Music for the struggling students is pure therapy! Students feeling positive about themselves are one of the major goals of a middle school. Music helps students feel good about themselves and good about life. Thus, success on a musical instrument is more than just a grade or a pat-on-the-back. Music performance creates a deep spiritual feeling for each student and says, "I am doing well and I feel good about myself."

~ ALICE ~

Alice was a 7th grader in one of my exploratory music classes. She has few friends, is often depressed but loves music and is very successful in my class on a day-to-day basis. My goal with Alice was to make her feel comfortable in the class, be sure she understood the material and encourage her to play for extra-credit as much as possible.

On the third week of class she purchased her own drum sticks at the local music store which was a major effort for her. Her test grades were excellent, and she enjoyed performing on the drum set. This was a joy for me as I would see Alice daily in the hallways moving slowly and always alone. I knew she was struggling academically, emotionally and socially. With her successes in my percussion class, I knew there was at least one class that she would look forward to from week to week. Her smile told the whole story at the end of each class and she never hesitated to perform solos for extra credit.

It was my continued work with struggling students like Alice that gave me the insight and the motivation to see the spiritual side of every child. Every child has talent, but it is in a treasure chest. To open each struggling child's treasure chest of talent there must be confidence on behalf of the teacher to encourage the child to stay in touch with their talent. With adequate time , coaching and practice on an instrument every struggling child in school can find their talent via the school owned instrument, the school schedule and the school music teacher.

~ ADRIENNE ~

Being shy and withdrawn, Adrienne was most reluctant to perform in my guitar class. She began by attempting to play the guitar backwards, but soon became used to the idea of using her left hand for the individual pitches, chords and bass lines. As the class began every day, I could see her begin slowly and appear very lost as the class proceeded with its warm-ups and new material for the day.

To make Adrienne more comfortable in class, I divided the class into groups of three with each person playing their choice of melody, chords and bass. I encouraged Adrienne to begin with the bass line, gradually try the chords and finally the bass. Working with two other girls in the class who were strong musicians, Adrienne joined in the trio performance and as a group member did very well.

Before the class ended, Adrienne was performing beautifully both with her trio and by herself as a soloist for extra-credit. Her confidence began to grow with each class and by the completion of the course her parent purchased a beginning level acoustic guitar for her. I considered this one of my biggest successes of the year as a teacher.

~ SARAH ~

Sarah was a foster child with a difficult background. She was verbally aggressive in the first guitar class and shut down emotionally refusing to do anything with the guitar. The next classes she was absent from school, but when she returned to class I found her very quiet and reserved. In the third week of class I noticed that one of our most talented music students in the class took an interest in Sarah and quickly became her mentor in the class.

Within two weeks I found Sarah working closely with ted, trying to do the extra-credit work and teaming well in her trio which included herself, ted and Brian. Sarah became more relaxed in the class, was able to go with the flow of the musical assignments and enjoyed teaming with the boys. I was proud of myself for not over-reacting to Sarah's disappointing first day of class. She was not sure of me as a new teacher in her schedule and I was sure she has had some bad times in her past with other teachers. Sensing all this, I was very pleased with Sarah, her accomplishments and the joy she expressed in the final classes of the grading period.

~ JOE ~

Joe was a disruptive student during the first six weeks of class. His distractions of other students were inappropriate and it was clear that he was able to control parents and other adults in his home life. However, as the course progressed for the second six weeks Joe and I had a number of talks. He began teaming with other students in the class who were embarrassed by Joe's behavior which would not be tolerated in their group.

Soon I discovered that Joe's father played guitar and would be willing to come to our class to perform. With great anticipation the class gave Joe's father a huge round of applause as he entered the music class on our final day together. His performance was a blend of country, blue grass, blues and rock 'n' roll. He performed during the entire class time and talked with the students about his experiences on the guitar and the multiple instruments he had purchased over the years.

I videotaped his performance and gave the tape to him as a small thank you from the school for his time and interest. Joe was most proud of his father and so were we all. Seldom do I have a student volunteer a parent to come to school to perform. This was a special moment and we all were very excited and grateful for the opportunity to share this time together.

~ ALEX ~

Wanting to perform, compose and organize his own group, Alex found himself very interested in guitar, voice and his own musical compositions. He found the traditional school program functional but not addressing his main focus in the field of music. As such, he began taking private lessons and over a three year period was singing, playing his guitar and performing. As private lessons continued to become more sophisticated, Alex progressed to more experienced teachers and he purchased more sophisticated equipment (guitar, amplifiers, speakers and microphone.)

As Alex progressed to the high school, there was little opportunity for him to perform or study composition. As such, he was most active in his musical pursuits outside the school day, but the traditional school music program gave him little to no opportunities as a guitarist.

It was clear to me that Alex could focus on the guitar, voice and music composition after high school. Alex taught me that school music programs need to address the excitement of student initiated bands, student initiated compositions and student initiated performances.

Alex was struggling. He felt alone with no in-school professionals caring about his talent and his love of music. I have shared the story of Alex and the lessons he taught me with many guitarists who seek musical guidance via music stores, older friends who are more experienced guitarists, or family members who play guitar and sing. This story changed our school program at the middle school level forever.

CHAPTER EIGHT

The Hurting Angels

Life at times seems so cruel and unfair, but I have managed to understand that such a viewpoint is very egotistical as God has a plan that is for a divine purpose. My role is just to follow my mission in life and be as helpful as possible to as many people I contact through my circle of influence. Finding my role and knowing that seeing God in the faces of the hurting angels has helped me to reach out to these struggling angels with all my love, caring and passion as a caring listener to their individual struggles in life.

~ HEATHER ~

The life of Heather began falling apart in the 6th grade with low grades, few friends, control issues at home and a behavior that gradually became out of control. During my music classes Heather began with an attitude and seldom participated in the class activities, However, I made it a point before each class to make eye contact with her and say, "hello" to her without fail. As each class followed I heard her call my name and I was sure that I made eye contact with her with a pleasant greeting.

As our music class progressed, I noticed that she was absent from school many consecutive days and at one point was suspended from school. When she returned to class I made sure she knew she was missed. I wondered how many other teachers or adults outside of school were giving Heather many positive attention and positive reinforcement. As we approached the final days of the grading period, I gave the class one final test. Heather had done above average on the first test but missed the next two tests due to absences. This test would be important to her final grade for the grading period.

On the day of the final test I was pleased to see Heather in school. Heather not only did well on the testing, she received one of the highest grades in the class plus completed the extra credit portion. The entire class gave Heather a round of applause when I read to them Heather's grade. When the report cards were distributed the following week, Heather was most proud of her "A" grade in music as her other grades were C's and D's with one F. Music brought out a positive side of Heather who was hurting and struggling in all her other classes.

~ MARSHALL ~

At times I meet a talented student who has no parental support at home, and in fact, lives with an older brother or sister. Such was the case with Marshall who wanted to play with our school band. Marshall was a sensitive student, bright, but was suffering from the aftermath of a brutal family situation and was removed from the family setting to live with his older sister who was 25 years old.

Marshall asked to play baritone horn in the band, and as the school provided these instruments for a very small annual fee, the family had no difficulty making the rental payment. Throughout the year Marshall struggled musically, he missed many days of school and his short attention span caused major rehearsal problems during the school day. I met with his older sister and Marshall together. She was very supportive of Marshall and was herself a flutist. We agreed that Marshall should have someone to one time with me after school and we set a time and a schedule that would work each week for the family.

As the weeks passed, Marshall became much more comfortable with the baritone horn, the rehearsals with the other kids (60 students in the band,) and with me as the conductor. At the end of the school year Marshall moved to a new school and did not continue his baritone horn, however, I thought that in the future he may be motivated to continue with music and his own band. I hope I meet up with Marshall someday and can hear a recording of his music.

~ KATHERINE ~

Some students have a wonderful musical talent, but the style of music they perform is of concern to parents, especially if the parents are very religious and very conservative in the points of view about life. Katherine suffered brutally from this scenario as she was a brilliant saxophone performer, pianist and singer. In the band she won all the high honors and won numerous medals and accolades from professional musicians, musical judges and professors of music.

As we approached the spring semester, Katherine approached me about starting her own band with her as the lead singer and pianist. I thought this was a great idea and encouraged her to contact those musicians in school with whom she would work well in a music-making venture. As she organized the group and began practicing, I felt that there was something missing about her performances. Finally, one day she told me that her mother did not approve of her singing popular music. She was motivated to write her own music and lyrics, but she had to keep all this creative effort out of the sight and listening of her parents at home.

At first I was devastated to hear such a lack of support for one of the most talented music students in school history. As our performance date approached, I was aware that Katherine and her group would be one of the best groups on the concert, but her parents would never want to hear her talent or creativity. As Katherine graduates and moves on in her life, my prayer is that her parents will find it in their heart to support her talent and the style of music that she can relate to at this young age of her musical life. I look forward to hearing from Katherine in the years ahead.

CHAPTER NINE

The Great Circle of Love:
Learning and Teaching

When is a teacher the teacher and the student the student, and when is the teacher the student and the student the teacher? This is THE GREAT CIRCLE OF LOVE. There are so many roles that each of us play from day to day. I marvel at watching very talented teachers in school being taught the latest techniques with the computer by one of their 6th grade students. In the martial arts I am always amazed at watching a 12 year-old black belt student teaching an adult who has a colored belt.

The teacher is the person with the information who wants to share it with others. The student is the person who wants the information from the teacher. What do you have if the student does not want to share the information and the student does not want to learn the information? This is daycare. This is babysitting.

Teaching 6th graders every day, I continue to be excited about the various learning styles involved at the beginning skill level of playing a musical instrument. Each student is encouraged to use both their vocal and listening skills during their first year. It is interesting to see how eager a beginning instrumentalist is at the ages of 10-12. many have waited years to begin an instrument, and others want to play the instrument one of their parents played when they were in school.

Over the years, I have improved my listening skills as the students progress from the traditional folk tunes in their beginning book to duets, rounds and trios. It is exciting to see the growth from "barnyard-type sounds" to the actual sounds of the instrument they are holding. Role-playing is an important teaching tool. When we role play, I play the student and the students play the teacher so each student can more clearly internalize the problem and then logically solve the problem with both knowledge and confidence.

I always find time in my classes to have solo performances. Students want to show what they can do, but as part of this format I always have the students evaluate the student performance. It is interesting to see how overly critical the students are of each other. It is important for the student of music to know that their primary instrument is their voice and their vocal skills are the model for their beginning instrumental skills to follow and imitate. The more experienced voice will always sound superior to the beginning instrumentalist; thus, students need to learn how to play both roles in this cameo production called "practicing your instrument at home."

As students progress from the beginning stages of performances through high school and college, they return to invite me to join them on their recital or give me their last recording. Suddenly, I find myself as the student listening to my former student inform me about the new literature being performed, the latest invention for their instrument or their purchase of a new instrument model I have never heard of in my entire life. This is how a teacher grows: "listening and learning from their students. being open to listen to and being open to learn from your former students is a joyous feeling that you, as the teacher, have contributed something significant in a human life forever! This is what sustains teachers.

Every student comes into your life with different cultural, religious and family values. Accepting this reality and helping each student progress in their skill development from day to day gives the teacher a feeling of accomplishment and significance. This never ending CIRCLE OF LOVE between the teacher and student is what gives one completeness, wholeness and satisfaction in life.

CHAPTER TEN

Discovering Your Soul: Loving the Children

Some of the most angelic sounds is children at play, children enjoying each other's company, children teaming together on a school project, performing in a school music group or performing on a sports team. There is a synergistic feeling of love, harmony and caring for each other that creates a euphoric feeling that is very "spiritual."

The great coaches of any team, academic, music, drama, dance or sport know that molding each individual attitude into a team attitude with synergistic skills will help the team succeed in reaching their goal. The passion, commitment and love of the discipline is the combination for success. The physical attributes of the skills involved is important but the main focus of each team member.

There are some coaches who believe and there are some coaches who know. Those coaches who know succeed in accomplishing their goals. Children likewise have a beautiful network of "knowing." Children have "spiritual knowing" about many things in their daily lives including: themselves, friends, family, pets and their friend's families. The "spiritual knowing" enable children to enjoy themselves, feel safe and find comfort in their home and in their community.

As students sequence through school, they traditionally move from teacher to teacher on a year to year basis and they increase their knowledge and skill development with each passing year. However, in the field of music, many students see the same teacher from elementary school through high school. Among these teachers are the string orchestra conductor, the band director and the choral director. If the school system is small, one music teacher may see students from K-12 in classroom music, strings, winds and choral. With larger systems, it is not uncommon for the string orchestra conductor to work with students from elementary school through high school. Private music tutors also work with students on the skills of a specific instrument from elementary through high school.

This experience of longevity with students and grade level sequencing over seven or eight years requires the teacher to reach out to the soul of the student. Both teacher and student need to work together as one soul. The child is changing rapidly in this transition period in life and what once worked with a child in the 6th grade does not work at all with the same child in the 9th grade. The child is becoming more independent and more in charge of his or her approach to learning as well as more self-confident. The teacher is able to step back and develop a less controlling style of teaching to allow the student to participate in the decision-making process towards higher level skills.

As the student progresses in the sequence from year to year, the student's priorities change rapidly with their hero choice changing from parents to teachers, friends and peer groups. Often the students who were so eager to play the violin in 6th grade are now casually enjoying the social aspect of being in and enjoying the orchestra in high school and just being near their friends. The key is for is for the students and teacher to develop a relationship where both care about each other more than their skill development and performance success. The teacher needs to be there for the students every day. This stability and caring will enhance the student commitment and skill development as there is a spiritual flow of caring that travels both directions. You become so spiritually interwoven that there is no need to think about the relationship. The relationship just is: 24 hours a day and 7 days a week.

Many teachers have the payoff of a lifetime when their former students visit them at older ages and share life's experiences since their days in the classroom together. At one local school in my community two teachers just retired. Each of them had taught in the same school for over 40 years! What memories they and their students must have.

Schools have always been a mirror of the families and their values in a local community. Achievement in academics, the arts and athletics in a school setting can only accelerate to the level that parents want to support the effort. Daily homework is a huge part of academics and daily practicing is a huge part of both music skills and athletic skills. To achieve at one's highest level one must work at it daily, but who will monitor the daily homework and daily practice?

Some educators would say that the real action in education is a "second shift" event (3:00 p.m. - 11:00 p.m.). This is where the homework and practicing takes place. Monday through Friday from 7:00 a.m. - 3: p.m. is for the most part very structured, required by law and respected by local communities; however, when the bell rings to end the formal legally required school day, the creative part of the day begins. Students with similar interests and talent are grouped together for team competitions (athletic, academic and artistic) and school service organizations.

What happens to children who cannot stay after school for activities and special help? What happens to the homework that does not have any supervision or caring? What happens to students who need and want help with their skills in the performing arts and/or athletic skills when there are no parents to pay for the tutoring, summer camps, special equipment and provide the constant traveling to tutors and practices? What happens to these students is they become discouraged, they give up on their talent, and they recognize that they are not going to achieve their goals in academics, the performing arts or athletics resulting in a change in their self-esteem.

Parents control the learning process in schools. Through 9th grade, parents need to help their child(ren) with daily homework. Without this effort students will struggle with their academic subjects.

Parents run schools. They run schools by electing school board members, attending and voicing opinions at school board meetings, joining PTO's and PTA's and volunteering for special events and projects at school. Parent involvement in the life of a school gives the school a triangular balance with the administration and teaching staff.

Success in school for every student depends on the level of synergy among the child, parent and teacher. When a balance of caring and loving for each other is reached in this triangle, all involved succeed and have a beautiful synergistic experience: The whole is greater than the sum of the parts.

I pray that every child may enjoy this balance in life.

CHAPTER ELEVEN

Peace of Mind: Listen to the Vision of the Children

When I think of all those children's stories and all the Disney movies, it is interesting to note that it was always the children who saved the town, saw through the politics or rescued the family or family pet. My Chinese friends always use the phrase "clear mindedness", and I have often thought that children in many situations have the most objective perspective. Children often have the most honesty and the most clear minded view of any given situation. Children can more easily "see the forest in spite of the trees."

Parents, teachers, community leaders and local politicians have much on their mind, but nothing has more priority than the security and safety of their respective families. There is much truth to the phrase "most adults live lives of quiet desperation." However, children should not be living in desperate situations where their safety and security are at risk.

Elementary children, middle school children, high school children and adult children have interesting and very helpful perspectives on specific aspects of life at specific times in their lives. With elementary children there are few worries in the problem-solving process. They are most clever and wonderful about play and the art of making things into games, play and fun. Laughter is the sound of heaven and young children do it best.

Middle school students are beginning to experience major changes physically, emotionally and psychologically, Almost everything in their environment appears to have different values and different levels of appeal. The student's perspective of parents, friends, school, church, community and their own self-image change dramatically during these years. They become excellent at evaluation and knowing everything that is wrong with their environment and the people that are within their circle if influence: parents, family members, teachers church leaders and community leaders.

Tolerance and patience with differences is not one of the strengths at this age. Consistency is the mantra for this age group. Change is extremely upsetting at this time of life. Changes in the weather, daily schedules, substitute teachers, canceled events and promises not kept can dramatically change a student's behavior. Physical appearance and competition are ever so important. If you need to know about the current "in things" on any topic, just ask a middle school student and they can bring you up to date in minutes and keep you current on all topics of interest on a weekly basis.

High school students are sensitive about their self-image. There is a distinct line between their perception of winners and losers, including: families, sport teams, music groups, teachers, academics and extra-curricular programs. It is the responsibility of adults who influence high school students to keep student opinions and ideas in perspective with the bigger picture. Neither winning nor losing is a life or death situation. Students find cliques in high school where everyone thinks alike, looks alike, and have many similar values on all topics. Students at this age become very competent, work a job, become very mobile and are looking for opportunities to travel out of the local community and spend time away from the clutches of mom and dad. Movie producers were very nervous with the advent of the home video rental business, but with the high school student interest in "getting out of the house" movie theaters are alive and well with movie producers catering to their interests.

Adult children can be very surprising. The twenties include many rides on the emotional roller coaster including marriage, children, divorce, jobs, loss of job, financial independence, graduate school and bankruptcy. Perceptions at this age can be helpful to families and at times parents see their adult children do many things that they would never think of doing. It is a time of change and discovering challenging problem-solving techniques on a wide variety of topics. Many parents find their biggest challenges in accepting their adult child's independence, life style and different views of life's basic principles and mores.

The creativity with an adult child in their twenties and their parents is that there is a 20+ year span of time between comparative experiences, and it is amazing how the world does change physically in twenty years. The key is for parents and adult children to see that the more important principles of life never change in any culture or at any time in history. This is a surprise and a rude awakening for many adult children in their twenties. Cars, housing, clothes, vacations, fitness, income and entertainment combine to create a new "gospel for survival and happiness." However, with time the adult child becomes 29 years old and the biological clock begins to sound like a gong! This is when the balance of life, adulthood and another's perspective may be the priority and discussed seriously for the first time.

The "rat race" of the twenties gives way to more serious and more spiritual concerns beginning with prioritizing the love of others, and a deeper look into one's self. Many individuals find themselves confronting serious deadlines or changes between ages 28-30. Being prepared that there is a strong probability of crisis management at this time of life may be helpful in accepting this transitional time in life's bigger picture.

With this transition of change, it is often surprising how different we see the situation as first the adult child, then as the parent and finally as the grandparent. How wonderful it is to learn from your children that there may be a different or better way to accomplish the same goal. We all have the same needs and same aspirations in life despite our name, our religion, our culture, our politics, our gender or our age.

When will we learn as a world culture that the unconditional love of each other and the sharing of our knowledge is the highest level of spiritual life? Learning from every child is one lesson we can all enjoy and through every child and every grandchild connect to our spiritual selves and stay on course with our mission in life.

God bless the children.

They keep our priorities in balance.

Their honesty, purity, and innocence touch us

and help us connect with what is important.

They remind us each day of the principles

and priorities in life.

CHAPTER TWELVE

Spiritual Happiness Will Bond All Civilizations Who Hear It

Between 1979 and 1993 my wife, Judie, and I adopted six wonderful children. The first child was Gary, age 8 from Connecticut whom we adopted in 1980. The next three children were adopted from Korea two years apart in 1983, 1985, and 1987 at three months of age: Jesse, Bill and Josh. In 1993 we adopted a brother and sister, Lukas and Catie, ages 5 and 2 from Columbia who had been separated for two years. In each situation there were some adults who thought our efforts were too challenging, others who thought we were putting ourselves at risk and others who were overwhelmed with international adoptions.

We considered these children a gift from God and an opportunity to bring children into our family who otherwise would have never seen life beyond orphanages and foster homes. There was a period of adjustment for everyone as each child entered the family. As parents, we had the most adjustments and found parent support groups to be most helpful. As we were adjusting to each adoption, we also worked with "Heal the Children" and opened our home to international children in crisis who needed medical care.

Working with the adoption and foster care process we were learning with each new child. The specialized medical care, legal paperwork and the processing was often overwhelming as was the variety of needs each child required.

To make the necessary adjustments, we joined adoption support groups where we could share our concerns and learn from the experiences of other parents. These adoption support groups included parents that were going through what we were experiencing and understanding the emotional roller coaster of daily life. These parent support groups met once per month with informal gatherings as needed.

With such an international family we find ourselves much more aware of international events, international politics, national heroes from different countries and cultural activities happening throughout the calendar year. In our community we have a variety of international families. The interaction within the community is encouraged and nurtured with a very natural and supportive attitude of openness and caring.

There is a spiritual feeling of acceptance among the families in our neighborhood despite obvious differences and I have often felt that this is the type of spirit that is needed worldwide. Accepting the reality that people of different cultures can positively agree to disagree does not mean disrespect. It simply means we agree to disagree on specific topics and understand that it is impossible for different cultures with different mores and a different history to agree on all topics. We need to accept this reality without anger or misunderstanding.

People of different cultures can respect the history of another's race or religious beliefs without going to war or avenging the behaviors of grandparents, great grandparents or great, great grandparents.

The primary goal for future generations will be to hear the "angelic harmony" of adults in all cultures working with their children as one universe of humanity. The universe is "one song." The ability of all future cultures and religions to understand this reality will be the most beautiful of all melodies. Each generation gives the next generation all they have and all they know.

On the topic of "basic principles" nothing is original with each new generation. All cultures and races agree on the basic concepts of right and wrong, and all want the same things for their families and friends; good health, long life, love, caring and sharing. It is all learned from the previous generation. Thus, when we see adults fighting civil wars and religious wars, we know that the motivation to fight has been learned from the previous generation who learned it from their parents in yet a previous generation.

As every new generation of children is taught by the previous generation of adults, each family is teaching their children how to raise their family with specific attitudes and beliefs about each aspect of life's challenges. This includes the quality of each child's physical health, personal hygiene, diet, education, religion, social mores and basic principles of right and wrong. This also includes developing attitudes about accepting differences in others.

The teachers of children can only give what they know. What they know is what they have lived. Teachers know that the superficial changes from generation to generation (popular music, clothing styles, fads and entertainment,) the basic human principles of success, abundance and happiness never change. We demonstrate our knowledge of these principles by our actions at home, at school, at our place of worship and in our community.

The heartbeat of our lives is based on these time-honored principles which we all clearly understand and were taught when we were children. Continuing to teach these principles to future generations is the highest spiritual calling for the present generation.

My prayer for future generations begins with a high priority: more positive role models and dedicated mentors for every child who will encourage and demonstrate to children how to accept the difference in individuals of all ages as well as the differences in their race, religion and culture. My prayer ends with the highest priority: that each child of each future generation will know that God lives within each of them and is calling for "one universal intelligence"; "one song of thought."

There are beautiful angels sounding beautiful tunes in our lives. These angels are repeatedly sounding the call for a spiritual course of action for all who will listen.

The question is "Are we prepared each day to listen and are we excited each day to hear the beautiful songs of joy, hope and love by the angels in our individual lives?"

ABOUT THE AUTHOR

 **Larry D. Allen** is presently Principal of Boone Grove Middle School in Boone Grove, Indiana. He has taught and conducted music programs and courses at the college and university level at the following institutions: Trinity College (Hartford, Connecticut), The Hartt School, Central Connecticut State University, Valparaiso University, VanderCook College of Music, Duquesne University, and Villanova University.

In 1981, Mr. Allen initiated SUMMER MUSIC INSTITUTES, a graduate level summer music program for music educators featuring the national and international talents in the field in K-12 music education as instructors. Over twenty years, this summer educational extravaganza expanded to five site locations under Mr. Allen's direction which attracts approximately 4,000 music educators each summer representing over one million public school students.

Since 1969, Mr. Allen has worked annually in public schools as a music educator and as a school administrator in Connecticut, Massachusetts, and

Indiana. He has received recognition for his unique public school music programs including: "The Artist-in-Residence Program," "The Side-by-Side Symphony Series," "Sound: The Physics of Music," and "The Exploratory Music Program."

As a graduate of Northmont High School in Clayton, Ohio, Mr. Allen received his Bachelor of Music Education Degree from Baldwin-Wallace College, his Masters of Music Degree in oboe performance with Robert Bloom and Bert Lucarelli at the Hartt School, and his Sixth Year Degree in Educational Administration from the University of Connecticut.

He has performed as an oboist and English hornist with symphony orchestras in Hartforrd, Connecticut, New Britain, Connecticut, Bridgeport, Connecticut, Worcester, Massachusetts, and LaPorte, Indiana.

He and his wife, Judie have adopted six children representing the State of Connecticut, and the countries of Korea and Colombia. Both have been leaders in the Open Door Society for Adoptive Families and Heal the Children providing international foster care.